OFFICIAL
FORTNITE
OUTFITS
COLLECTORS' EDITION

CONTENTS

OUTFITS AND SETS

Looking for a particular gear set? Here's where to find all of the Outfits and other items featured in this book!

FEATURES

Other gear, tips, FAQs, and more...

DRESS TO IMPRESS!

IT'S IMPORTANT TO LOOK YOUR BEST WHEN YOU JUMP FROM THE BATTLE BUS

THE EVER-GROWING COLLECTION OF OUTFITS IN FORTNITE HAS ALWAYS BEEN AN ESSENTIAL PART OF THE GAME'S IDENTITY AND POPULARITY. As the exclusive concept art here shows, image is everything when it comes to leaving your mark on a Battle Royale match.

But Outfits aren't just about fashion. They're also tools for psyching out enemies to allow you to strike in their moment of weakness. They're a way of telling other players something about yourself without having to say a word. Oh, and it doesn't hurt that so many of them look awesome!

As your wardrobe gets more and more packed with options as you purchase Outfits and check off Battle Pass Tiers, you're able to mix and match costumes with the various other cosmetic items to create an exponentially increasing variety of looks.

Your Fortnite fashion quest starts here, with a few tips for creating the perfect flex.

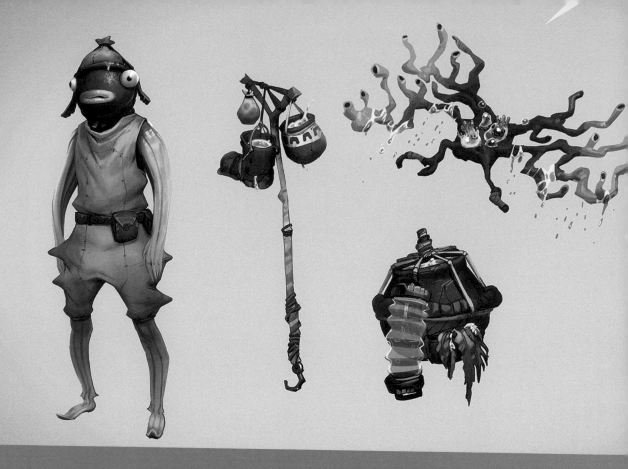

SOMETIMES, LESS IS MORE

THE SHEER VARIETY PRESENT IN FORTNITE'S MANY OUTFITS MEANS THAT THERE'S SOMETHING FOR EVERYONE, AND A LOOK FOR ALL OCCASIONS.

If you want to dress up in a wacky full-body costume, then go for it, but if you'd rather drop in wearing something a little more reserved, that's cool, too! The same goes for other cosmetic items such as Back Blings and Harvesting Tools—even the simplest of these can be the perfect finishing touch for the look you're trying to create.

WORKING WITH SETS

YOU DON'T ALWAYS HAVE TO BE WILDLY CREATIVE WHEN COMBINING ITEMS TO MAKE A LOOK.

Some sets—such as Fishstick's awesome Fish Food set, as seen in this early concept art above—work so well together that just using the full set is often the way to go. Sets are the easiest way to theme your look and make sure you stick to it.

KEEP AN EYE ON THE STORE

YOU CAN FIND INSPIRATION IN ALL KINDS OF PLACES, INCLUDING THE ITEM SHOP. Check out new Outfits, as you may find their Back Bling or other bundled items would be perfect for another Outfit you love using. For instance, Dusk's gothic look can be made even creepier by equipping Lace's evil teddy bear Back Bling, Stitches.

FORTNITE JUST KEEPS EVOLVING

WITH NEW CONTENT ADDED TO THE GAME EVERY SINGLE WEEK, AND RADICAL CHANGES COMING IN WITH EVERY NEW SEASON, FORTNITE NEVER STAYS STILL FOR LONG. We strived to make the contents of this book accurate at the time of printing, but it's possible that certain details have changed by the time you read this. That's just how fast the game moves!

ADVANCED FORCES
GRAB YOUR FATIGUES AND ROLL OUT, SOLDIER!

SLEDGEHAMMER

INTRODUCED IN: SEASON 5
RARITY: EPIC

SLEDGEHAMMER IS A SKIN MADE FOR CAMOUFLAGE IN DESERT COMBAT. The Advanced Forces set is one of the hardest collections to complete. Three of its items, including the True North backpack, have only been available to Twitch Prime subscribers, while others like this have been locked behind the higher ends of Battle Passes.

UPLINK

BATTLEHAWK

INTRODUCED IN: SEASON 4
RARITY: EPIC

IT TAKES A CERTAIN KIND OF PERSON TO BE ABLE TO PULL OFF AN EYEPATCH. Choosing to limit one's own depth perception when heading into combat is either very brave or very stupid (or both), but if you're going to bag yourself a Royale, you want to look good doing it, right? Battlehawk's armored vest has seen better days, but it certainly ties up his military-themed look nicely, and sometimes that's enough.

SQUAD LEADER

INTRODUCED IN: SEASON 4
RARITY: EPIC

THE PERFECT LOOK TO HELP YOU RALLY THE TROOPS. Locked to the top end of the premium Battle Pass, this smart skin required you to grind to get it, but if you did, you got one of the coolest Outfits in the game. You even get an awesome full sleeve tattoo to give it an extra layer of swagger!

STANDARD
ISSUE

TRAILBLAZER

INTRODUCED IN: SEASON 4
RARITY: EPIC

A GREAT SKIN IF YOU DON'T WANT TO CREATE TOO MUCH OF A FUSS. Another advantage of using this skin is how similar it looks to the default skins. This means you could potentially fool players into thinking you are new to Fortnite, when actually you are an expert who can hit sniper headshots from 200 meters. Of course you are...right?

AEROSOL ASSASSINS
TAG YOUR WAY TO A VICTORY ROYALE

ABSTRAKT

INTRODUCED IN: SEASON 4
RARITY: EPIC

READY TO LEAVE YOUR MARK ON THE ISLAND? Grab your paint cans, load up on your best Sprays, and get to tagging everything in sight—but remember that smart opponents might be able to follow your trail of art if you get *too* creative.

TEKNIQUE

INTRODUCED IN: SEASON 4
RARITY: EPIC

NOT QUITE PAINT-BY-NUMBERS, TEKNIQUE WALKS ON THE WILD SIDE. This Outfit has paint everywhere: the gloves, leggings, shoes, and even the hoodie's forearms are covered in spots of acrylic. The dry-cleaning bills on this streetwise getup must be a nightmare.

TAG BAG

10

A.I.M.

ELIMINATING HUMAN ERROR, ONE HUMAN AT A TIME

E.L.I.M.

A.I.M.

INTRODUCED IN: SEASON 6
RARITY: LEGENDARY

OUTFITS THAT ARE AWARDED FOR COMPLETING SKILL-BASED CHALLENGES OFTEN GO ON TO BE SOME OF THE MOST POPULAR IN THE GAME. As such, expect to see A.I.M. becoming a more and more common pick for those who have it over the coming seasons, if only to upset those who don't—and now most likely never will. We're suckers for robots, and A.I.M.'s simple design is clean and cool.

FACT

A.I.M. is one of only a handful of skins that is not a person in a costume—the mechanical midriff makes it pretty clear that this thing is all machine!

> "I LIKE THE FACT THAT THEY ADDED PANTS ON THIS ONE!"
> **LASERBOLT, YOUTUBE**

ANIMAL JACKETS
THROWING DOWN WITH HOODS UP

NIBBLES

FLAPJACKIE

INTRODUCED IN: SEASON 6
RARITY: EPIC

FLAPJACKIE IS A RABBIT. At least, it's meant to be. The big ears and tag make it look like a giant version of a cuddly toy gone horribly, *horribly* wrong. Flapjackie is designed for those who want to look like the trendiest pet around. Bonus points, too, for the skin coming with a cutesy stuffed rabbit called Nibbles.

GROWLER

INTRODUCED IN: SEASON 6
RARITY: EPIC

WHO DOESN'T WANT TO LOOK LIKE A RAZOR-TOOTHED MONSTER BEING EATEN BY A PLUSH POOCH? This curious costume definitely sits at the stranger end of Fortnite's closet, and while it's anything but subtle, it should at least instill a little fear in those who see it coming. Just make sure your bark isn't worse than your bite!

WOOFS

APEX PROTOCOL
BET YOU WISH YOU LOOKED THIS GOOD IN ORANGE...

VERTEX

INTRODUCED IN: SEASON 4
RARITY: LEGENDARY

ONE OF THE COOLEST SKINS FROM SEASON 4, VERTEX IS TYPICALLY RESERVED FOR SERIOUS FANS. It's part of the very sleek and stylish Apex Protocol set, and purchasing it also unlocks the cool Deflector Back Bling, an understated way to make the Outfit's armor appear a little chunkier.

FACT
The Apex Protocol set also includes the amazing Forerunner Glider and an unusually shaped pickaxe known as Razor Edge. A particularly desirable set.

DEFLECTOR

FORERUNNER

ARACHNE

INTRODUCED IN: SEASON 6
RARITY: LEGENDARY

THERE AREN'T MANY FORTNITE SKINS THAT CAN SCARE AN OPPONENT INTO SUBMISSION, BUT THE SPIDERY ARACHNE MAY DO THE TRICK.

If the creepy red eyes on the mask don't make you run for the (haunted) hills, then the Back Bling—the suitably named Long Legs—might just finish the job. The eight-legged metallic Back Bling was also introduced during Season 6's Halloween event and, much like the costume it comes paired with, makes you look like one giant, nasty creepy-crawly.

> "OH MY GOODNESS! THAT'S KINDA CREEPY!"
> **VALKYRAE, TWITCH**

LONG LEGS

INTRODUCED IN: SEASON 6
RARITY: LEGENDARY

IF YOU MISSED THE BLACK KNIGHT OUTFIT BACK IN SEASON 2, NOW'S YOUR CHANCE TO GET YOUR HANDS ON THE NEXT BEST THING. Spider Knight is a little creepier than its medieval cousin, with extra red eyes on the helmet and tattered armor to help hammer home the gloomy theme. Arachne's Long Legs Back Bling can really set off this awesome Outfit and make it a nightmare to deal with for anyone who doesn't like bugs!

SPIDER SHIELD

WEB BREAKER

ARCHETYPE
WHAT IS BEHIND THAT STRANGE MASK?

ARCHETYPE

INTRODUCED IN: SEASON 5
RARITY: EPIC

RELEASED AS A SET ALONG WITH THE PARADIGM BACK BLING, THIS HI-TECH SOLDIER ISN'T MESSING AROUND.
Adorned with a bandolier of custom heavy rounds on his shoulder, Archetype's appearance brings an uneasy presence to the battlefield. This Outfit shines when combined with the Servo Glider, the final part of the Archetype set, which deploys a neon-green mechanical glider that will see you soar down in style....

PARADIGM

ARCTIC COMMAND
CHILL OUT IN THESE COOL OUTFITS

ICE BREAKER

ABSOLUTE ZERO

INTRODUCED IN: SEASON 2
RARITY: RARE

WITH SO MANY BRIGHT AND COLORFUL OUTFITS IN THE GAME, SIMPLE ONES LIKE THIS ARE OFTEN A BREATH OF FRESH AIR. Absolute Zero is a stylish monochrome Outfit that predates the arrival of Polar Peak by a good five seasons, but there are few better costumes for exploring those snowy slopes.

ARCTIC ASSASSIN

INTRODUCED IN: SEASON 2
RARITY: RARE

SOME OUTFITS ONLY MAKE RARE APPEARANCES IN THE ITEM SHOP, BUT THIS FROSTY NUMBER IS QUITE THE OPPOSITE. Arctic Assassin has been available for purchase at least once per month ever since its release in January 2018, so nobody needs to miss out on this understated Outfit.

AVIATION AGE
STEAMPUNK SKYFARERS SOAR INTO ACTION!

AIRHEART

INTRODUCED IN: SEASON 6
RARITY: RARE

YOU'VE GOT TO LOVE A BIT OF FORESHADOWING! These pilots were planeless when they first arrived on the island, but the very next season, they got to take to the skies in the X-4 Stormwing. This smart skin's name is a reference to flight pioneer Amelia Earhart—the first female pilot to fly solo across the Atlantic, in 1928.

TURBINE

CLOUDBREAKER

INTRODUCED IN: SEASON 7
RARITY: RARE

WE THINK POOR OLD CLOUDBREAKER HAS PROBABLY LOST MORE THAN A FEW PAIRS OF REGULAR GOGGLES TO TURBULENT WINDS. Still, he won't be losing any more now they're firmly attached to his face as part of a larger mask. This practical solution doubles as a striking look that will make foes stop and take notice, too.

MAXIMILIAN

INTRODUCED IN: SEASON 6
RARITY: RARE

NEED AN ACE PILOT ON YOUR SQUAD?

Everyone does! Maximilian's sharp suit and vintage flight helmet make this perhaps the most understated Outfit in the set. If you want to make it a bit bolder, there are plenty of Back Bling options that can do the job—find one you like and run with it!

AIRFLOW

WINGTIP

INTRODUCED IN: SEASON 7
RARITY: RARE

WITH HER CADET'S CAP AND PROMINENT SLEEVE PATCHES, WINGTIP LOOKS LIKE SHE JUST LANDED STRAIGHT FROM THE FLIGHT ACADEMY. She clearly shares Cloudbreaker's love of a nice fleecy jacket to stave off the cold at higher altitudes. Wingtip offers a strong look for anyone looking to soar towards a Victory Royale.

BIKER BRIGADE
RIDE TOGETHER, WIN TOGETHER

BACKBONE

INTRODUCED IN: SEASON 5
RARITY: RARE

A FEARSOME BIKER LOOK IS THE BACKBONE OF THIS SKIN. Talk to your friends, synchronize this look with them, and turn up as a dominating biker gang. Get yourself a Throttle Harvesting Tool to keep the theme on the straight road. Now it's really a race to the final circle, and you're ready to ride in style.

CHOPPER

INTRODUCED IN: SEASON 5
RARITY: RARE

TAKE A BREAK FROM THE HIGHWAY TO DROP FROM THE BATTLE BUS. In black and red, with plenty of leather and studs, Chopper is a hardcore member of a biker gang. The Road Ready or Road Flair Back Bling items make this Outfit stand out further. She might look out of place pushing a shopping cart, but she'll always appear cool and tough.

ROAD FLAIR

BLACK VECTOR
WHY LOOK THIS GOOD IF NO ONE IS SUPPOSED TO SEE YOU?

ELITE AGENT

INTRODUCED IN: SEASON 3
RARITY: EPIC

SHHHH, DO YOU HEAR SOMETHING? Of course you don't—the Elite Agent is a master of covert operations, and can break into any fortress. Once the sun goes down, this Outfit makes it easy to sneak up on enemies, eliminate any threats, and rescue downed teammates. Equip other items from the set like the Carbon Glider or Tactical Spade to round out this ultimate stealth package.

ROGUE AGENT

INTRODUCED IN: SEASON 5
RARITY: EPIC

AN EARLY FAVORITE OF THOSE WHO PURCHASED THE EPIC STARTER PACK. Rogue Agent gives you a bit of mystique and swagger on the field. It's a great Outfit if you like to have your character's face covered, and the black skintight costume is perfect for lurking in the shadows and leaping out at unsuspecting foes. This secret-agent-themed set is easily one of the coolest in the game.

BUSHIDO
SHOGUNS WITH SHOTGUNS

HIME

INTRODUCED IN: SEASON 5
RARITY: LEGENDARY

THE STRIKING HIME OUTFIT DRAWS FROM ANCIENT JAPANESE CULTURE. Featuring a horned helmet and animal mask to help unnerve your enemies, this skin is sure to make you stand out. *Hime* translates into English as "Princess," but this princess needs no knight to rescue her.

PURRFECT

MUSHA

INTRODUCED IN: SEASON 5
RARITY: LEGENDARY

BRING FEUDAL JAPAN TO TILTED TOWERS WITH A SKIN THAT FOCUSES ON TRADITION. *Musha* means "Warrior" in Japanese, with this samurai sporting blinged-out armor and a scary demonic mask. Trimmed with gold, the Musha skin is both regal and outlandish.

CALCULATOR CREW
ADD VICTORIES BY SUBTRACTING FOES

PAPER PLANE

MAVEN

INTRODUCED IN: SEASON 7
RARITY: RARE

YOU SHOULDN'T NEED A CALCULATOR TO FIGURE OUT HOW MANY PEOPLE NEED TO BE LEFT STANDING AT THE END TO EARN YOU A VICTORY ROYALE. Still, if you want to show your work, this Outfit comes with more pens and pencils than you'll know what to do with.

PRODIGY

INTRODUCED IN: SEASON 7
RARITY: RARE

DO YOU LOVE MATH? Like, *really* love it, to the point that you'd wear a vest covered in mathematical symbols? Then meet your new BFF. Prodigy was exclusive to PlayStation Plus subscribers for a limited time, so the probability of seeing him running around is actually fairly low.

23

CARBIDE
AN EVOLVING HERO FOR AN EVOLVING GAME

INTRODUCED IN: SEASON 4
RARITY: LEGENDARY

BACK IN SEASON 4, CARBIDE WAS THE SKIN THAT SEEMINGLY EVERYONE HAD. With more and more players buying the Battle Pass and Carbide being a fixed reward just for starting out, everyone had access to the basic-version skin, and its awesome looks made it a popular choice for many.

Of course, as with most Battle Pass Tier 1 Outfits, you could complete challenges to unlock new skin styles, which in this instance come in the form of new armor pieces that can be layered over the original suit to bulk it out.

"EVERYTHING LOOKS BULKY... IT LOOKS SUPER GOOD."
EXOTIC EXO, YOUTUBE

POSITRON

FACT
The Carbide and Omega skins are very similar in looks, but with the latter requiring a Tier 100 Battle Pass to unlock, the former is a much more common sight.

Players who managed to reach Battle Pass Tier 65 were able to unlock all of the additional armor, transforming Carbide from a hero in a skintight suit into a massive, fully-armored combat machine. Completing the first three challenges also unlocked the Positron pickaxe to complete the set.

This theme of Outfits that evolve as players perform well with them has become increasingly popular in recent seasons, and Carbide was one of the first examples. Without him, we'd miss so many of the cool costumes we see today. Thanks, buddy!

CHOMP
WE'RE GONNA NEED A BIGGER BATTLE BUS

LASER CHOMP

CHOMP SR.

INTRODUCED IN: SEASON 5
RARITY: LEGENDARY

IF YOU'RE LOOKING TO UNLEASH YOUR INNER SHARK, CHOMP SR. IS FOR YOU.
It comes with a fitting Back Bling to go along with the suit: a giant shark fin. You can complete your sharktastic collection by dropping some more V-Bucks on Chomp Jr.—a shark-themed Harvesting Tool that is just adorable. Well, as adorable as a shark can be, anyway....

FACT
A group of sharks is called a "shiver," so now you know what to call yourselves when you and your friends all drop into Squads wearing the Chomp Sr. Outfit!

COBRA CREW
SNAKE, RATTLE, AND ROLL INTO ACTION

MAVERICK

INTRODUCED IN: SEASON 5
RARITY: EPIC

THE WORD "MAVERICK" MEANS AN UNORTHODOX OR INDEPENDENT-MINDED PERSON. Like the Moniker and Fortune skins—both seem to be modeled on modern fashion—Maverick is a cool guy. Pair this up with the Bat Attitude Back Bling and you're well equipped to be the most cantankerous hoodlum the Fortnite map has ever seen.

CLUTCH AXE

SHADE

INTRODUCED IN: SEASON 5
RARITY: EPIC

YOU MIGHT THINK THIS IS JUST A NORMAL OUTFIT FOR ANY YOUNG PERSON WALKING THE STREETS OF YOUR HOMETOWN. No, Shade is just one of the game's more understated Epic skins. It's a nice combination of studded aggression and a casual hoodie, complete with a fetching haircut. It's a fairly low-key skin, and as part of the Cobra Crew set, it features...well, a cobra. Who *are* this Cobra Crew, exactly?

CRITERION
TOMORROW'S BATTLE ROYALE PARTICIPANT, TODAY!

CRITERION

INTRODUCED IN: SEASON 4
RARITY: LEGENDARY

THE CRITERION SKIN DEMANDS UNWAVERING DEDICATION TO THE BATTLE ROYALE CAUSE.
The blue-and-orange color scheme and the armored angles of the suit design give it a real superhero feel, and it's a little reminiscent of the Carbide skin from Season 4's beginning.

It launched alongside the rather dark and foreboding aesthetic of the Oblivion Outfit, which comes bundled with the Destabilizer Back Bling, designed to be the color-based opposite of Criterion's much brighter Stabilizer pack.

STABILIZER

Like many skins in recent seasons, the Criterion outfit is available as a bundle which includes the Stabilizer Back Bling for no extra cost. They make one futuristic-looking combo!

TRICERA OPS & REX

INTRODUCED IN: SEASON 3
RARITY: LEGENDARY

TERRORIZE THE BATTLEFIELD WITH THESE MONSTROUS DINOSAUR COSTUMES. The Rex Outfit is a classic, and has been a fan favorite since it first appeared. Tricera Ops, meanwhile, is a much bolder statement for anyone who feels like getting prehistoric on the competition. Unleash the beasts!

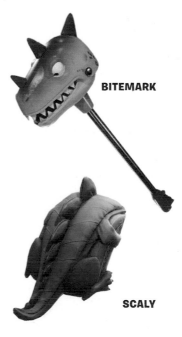

BITEMARK

SCALY

TRAILBLAZERS

MAKE A GREAT FIRST IMPRESSION WITH ONE OF THESE AWESOME CONTRAILS

WHEN YOU FIRST LEAVE THE BATTLE BUS AND START PLUMMETING INTO THE FORTNITE MAP, IT'S ESSENTIAL THAT YOU LET EVERYONE KNOW JUST HOW STYLISH YOU ARE. Before the other players even see your character, they'll see whatever trail you choose to leave in your wake as you dive onto the island, and that can be anything from molten lava to a colony of bats! Here's a selection of cool Contrail effects to show off your style before the first shot is even fired.

VINES

INTRODUCED IN: SEASON 7
RARITY: RARE

Leave a tangled trail of leaves, shoots, and roots behind you with this all-natural Contrail. Fans of the Flytrap Outfit shouldn't be without this one!

GLITCH IN THE SYSTEM

INTRODUCED IN: SEASON 5
RARITY: RARE

It was prophesied that only The One could equip this trail. Turns out that prophecy was wrong, and thousands of players have access. Who knew?

TP

INTRODUCED IN: SEASON 5
RARITY: RARE

A favorite of high-school pranksters. The sort of Contrail you'd equip if you were really on a roll, or if you wanted to wipe the floor with the competition.

SHOOTING STAR

INTRODUCED IN: SEASON 4
RARITY: RARE

Like a celestial body plummeting to earth, you'll put stars in the eyes of your opponents if you enter orbit with this Contrail. A real space oddity.

ICE CRYSTALS

INTRODUCED IN: SEASON 5
RARITY: RARE

Plummeting in with this cool trail is guaranteed to leave others feeling cold. Has been known to receive a frosty reception from new players.

LIGHTNING

INTRODUCED IN: SEASON 4
RARITY: RARE

A favorite tactic of players rocking this crackling trail is aiming for the tallest spot on the map and barreling toward it at breakneck speed. Flashy.

RETRO SCI-FI

INTRODUCED IN: SEASON 4
RARITY: RARE

The trail of choice for fans of old-school B-movies and weird old alien technology. Who doesn't want to shoot bright-green lasers from their hands?

HEARTS

INTRODUCED IN: SEASON 4
RARITY: RARE

You can literally leave a trail of broken hearts behind you as you stream through the air with this trail. A favorite for performing Cupid's stunts.

JACK-O-LANTERN

INTRODUCED IN: SEASON 6
RARITY: RARE

It can be Halloween every day of the year when you dive into action with a pair of blazing pumpkins. Only it can't—that's not how the calendar works.

RAINBOW

INTRODUCED IN: SEASON 3
RARITY: RARE

A lovely, friendly trail that players are proud to sport. Just don't expect it to lead you to a pot of gold when you land or you may end up disappointed!

SPRAY PAINT

INTRODUCED IN: SEASON 4
RARITY: RARE

A messy, unpredictable trail used by degenerates to mark their territory over the skies of the Battle Royale map. Famously bad for the ozone layer.

FLAMES

INTRODUCED IN: SEASON 3
RARITY: RARE

Hot stuff, coming through! This trail has you burning through the sky at extreme temperatures. Just remember to stop, drop, and roll when you land.

ALL-STAR

INTRODUCED IN: SEASON 3
RARITY: RARE

Anyone rocking this snazzy trail is an all-star, known for getting their game on. The sort of person who likes to be the star of the show.

EXHAUST

INTRODUCED IN: SEASON 6
RARITY: RARE

If you're in a hurry to touch down and start looting, why not try strapping jet engines to your arms to speed up your descent?

TRAILS IN THE SKY

A late development from Epic?

Contrails were not included in Fortnite Battle Royale at launch. Instead, the streaming effects were introduced in Season 3's Battle Pass, to a great reception. Many players had been keen for more customization options, and by the time Epic decided this was another cool way of letting players experiment with styles, the appetite for new items was at its peak. You can see how Epic has gotten more experimental with its designs as the seasons have progressed.

DIVEMASTERS
IN SEARCH OF DEEP COVER

REEF RANGER

INTRODUCED IN: SEASON 5
RARITY: EPIC

IT'S RARE THAT A SKIN FEELS INCOMPLETE WITHOUT A BACK BLING, BUT THAT IS EXACTLY THE CASE HERE. Without the Air Tank that comes bundled with it, you are going to look a little silly, because when you dive underwater you will have no air to breathe! Still, seeing the flippers slap onto the dirt as you run toward the circle is always satisfying.

WRECK RAIDER

INTRODUCED IN: SEASON 5
RARITY: EPIC

DO YOUR WEAK GLIDING SKILLS ALWAYS SEE YOU PLUMMET INTO THE DRINK WHEN YOU DROP IN? Take precautions by equipping this practical diving suit—at least you can give the impression you meant to make a splash. Combine this with Beef Boss' Deep Fried Back Bling to make it look like he's guzzling fries down those tubes!

DOUBLE HELIX
ARCHETYPE SWITCHES UP HIS COLORS

TELEMETRY

DOUBLE HELIX

INTRODUCED IN: SEASON 6
RARITY: EPIC

THERE'S NOTHING QUITE LIKE THE FEELING OF CRACKING OPEN THE BOX OF A BRAND-NEW CONSOLE. What could make that even better, you ask? Well...how about finding a code for a super-rare Fortnite Outfit in the box as well? Yeah, that'd do it. Double Helix's exclusive nature has made it one that fans really want to get their hands on, and it's certainly one of the most visually striking costumes in the game.

FACT
Being a bundle exclusive, Double Helix proved extremely desirable. The download code from the Switch pack alone has been known to sell for well over $100!

DRIFT
DRESS TO IMPRESS AND OUTFOX YOUR ENEMIES

DRIFT

INTRODUCED IN: SEASON 5
RARITY: LEGENDARY

DRIFT HAS PROVEN A VERY POPULAR SKIN, PROBABLY BECAUSE IT WAS INCLUDED AS A TIER 1 REWARD IN THE SEASON 5 BATTLE PASS. What makes Drift so interesting, though, are the various extra layers and additions you can unlock as you gain XP.

At first, these cosmetic upgrades are minor, but eventually you unlock a mask that completely changes the entire dynamic of the costume, turning it from a fairly plain look into something otherworldly.

It takes a lot of play to unlock every element, but Drift is a great example of how Fortnite Outfits have evolved since the early seasons, and we can expect more customizable skins in the future.

"OH, I LIKE IT WITH THE JACKET! I'M SO READY FOR SEASON 5, BRO!"
MYTH, TWITCH

We've already started to see a lot more progressive Outfits added as part of various Battle Passes, as well as some other novel ways of changing the way they can look. These are getting crazier, too, leaving players to wonder what could be coming next.

Best of all, though, is that Outfits such as Drift allow you to get invested in the characters. Your new favorite Outfit could be just a couple of thousand XP away!

RIFT EDGE

FACT

Drift's inclusion in the Battle Pass means he's unlikely to return for those who missed out. Luckily, the progressive Outfits that have been added since are just as awesome!

[URRR BURGER
BATTLE ROYALE WITH CHEESE

FLYING SAUCER

DURRR BURGER WRAP

B EF BOSS

INTRODUCED IN: SEASON 5
RARITY: EPIC

PART OF ITS OWN FAST FOOD-FLAVORED SET, THIS SKIN LOOKS GREAT COMBINED WITH THE DEEP FRIED BACK BLING AND PATTY WHACKER TOOL. Nobody will take you seriously in this Outfit, with its mismatched colors, tiny bow tie, and polka-dot patterns. That's before they've noticed you have a burger for a head. Imagine this being the last thing you see before being sent back to the lobby. Those googly eyes are absolutely terrifying.

FACT
Beef Boss is the mascot of the Durrr Burger fast-food chain, located in Greasy Grove from launch until Season 6 and later moved to Retail Row.

GRILL SERGEANT

INTRODUCED IN: SEASON 5
RARITY: UNCOMMON

GET IT? It's a pun on Drill Sergeant, and they shoot guns, too. This guy is more focused on delivering orders than pain, as he's decked out in a fast-food chef's attire. The hat and apron are perfect for serving up justice, and that headset could mean either calling in backup or requesting an extra serving of fries for table four.

DEEP FRIED

PATTY WHACKER

ONESIE

INTRODUCED IN: SEASON 7
RARITY: EPIC

MOST WOULD-BE SOLDIERS UNDERGO YEARS OF TRAINING BEFORE HEADING INTO COMBAT. But some would rather just roll out of bed and right into the action. This comfy-looking getup is certainly going to turn a few heads, at least so long as you only *look* like you've just woken up and don't play like it, too!

EON
A FUTURISTIC CONSOLE EXCLUSIVE TO MAKE YOUR ENEMIES GREEN WITH ENVY

RESONATOR

EON

INTRODUCED IN: SEASON 6
RARITY: LEGENDARY

WHAT BETTER LOOK FOR A CONSOLE TIE-IN OUTFIT THAN AN ADVANCED PIECE OF TECHNOLOGY? This sleek, clean look might be a re-skin of the Criterion Outfit, but it's a stark contrast to that much more vibrant skin—the black-and-white armor with luminous green accents helps it feel even more futuristic and lends it a distinctly Xbox flavor.

FACT
Seen this Xbox exclusive running around on other platforms? Thanks to cross-play and linked accounts, you might just come up against one, if you haven't already!

AURORA

FLOWER POWER
SHOW YOUR FOES SOME TOUGH LOVE

DREAMFLOWER

INTRODUCED IN: SEASON 5
RARITY: EPIC

THE DREAMFLOWER SKIN HARKS BACK TO THE 60s. This is a look seen around Woodstock in 1969 when everyone wore flowers in their hair and painted peace signs on their faces. A very groovy Outfit, especially for the more laid-back players out there.

SUMMER STRUMMER

FAR OUT MAN

INTRODUCED IN: SEASON 5
RARITY: EPIC

EQUIP THE TIE-DYE FLYER GLIDER AND DRIFT DOWN TO THE BATTLEFIELD ON WAVES OF PEACE AND LOVE. This hippie, decked out with trademark long hair and sunglasses, may seem more harmony and unity than build and outgun, but he can still pull his weight!

FLYTRAP

INTRODUCED IN: SEASON 4
RARITY: LEGENDARY

THERE ARE PLENTY OF STRIKING OUTFITS AVAILABLE IN FORTNITE, BUT THERE ARE FEW QUITE SO VIVID AND CREATIVE AS FLYTRAP. This green-fingered super-villain casts an imposing silhouette, with sharp tendrils and mandibles jutting off from all parts of his bodysuit, reminiscent of the carnivorous plant from which he gets his name. It's the sort of thing you wear when you want people to notice you, so you'd better have a killer monologue ready when they do (bonus points if you reveal the entirety of your evil plan for no reason).

A literal force of nature, Flytrap is here to stay, although he's a rare visitor to the Item Store so you'll likely have time to harvest V-Bucks before he's next ripe for the plucking.

"LOOK AT THIS SKIN! VINES COME OFF OF EVERYTHING THAT I DO—IT'S KINDA LIT!"
POKIMANE, TWITCH

VENUS FLYER

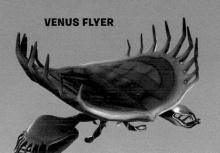

BLACK KNIGHT

INTRODUCED IN: SEASON 2
RARITY: LEGENDARY

ONE OF THE FIRST TRULY SCARY OUTFITS IN BATTLE ROYALE. When you saw this imposing figure, you knew it meant the opponent was a serious player. Up against a Black Knight? Well, you'd better know how to build, shoot, and, quite honestly, how to run away!

SQUIRE SHIELD

BLUE SQUIRE

INTRODUCED IN: SEASON 2
RARITY: RARE

AH, THE MEMORIES. Back in Season 2, when Battle Royale was still fairly new, the Blue Squire skin was all the rage. As a Tier 1 reward for the Battle Pass, a lot of committed Fortnite warriors could be seen running around the field with this suit of armor on, causing mischief, building bases, and throwing grenades.

RED KNIGHT

INTRODUCED IN: SEASON 2
RARITY: LEGENDARY

AN ALTERNATIVE TO THE BLACK KNIGHT FOR THOSE WHO DIDN'T MANAGE TO GET HIM FROM THE BATTLE PASS. This female version of the daunting armor-clad knight still pops up in the Item Shop from time to time, so be sure to grab it when you can if you're still searching for your knight in shining armor.

SIR GLIDER THE BRAVE

CRIMSON AXE

ROYALE KNIGHT

INTRODUCED IN: SEASON 2
RARITY: RARE

PLAYERS WHO MADE A LITTLE PROGRESS WITH THEIR SEASON 2 BATTLE PASSES GOT TO RUN AN EQUAL-OPPORTUNITIES ROUND TABLE. If you think these two Rare Outfits look pretty similar, good luck trying to tell their associated Back Bling items apart—the Squire Shield and the Royale Shield look identical!

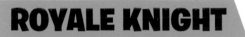

DISCO BALL

DISCO DIVA

INTRODUCED IN: SEASON 7
RARITY: RARE

WITH ALL OF THE DANCING CHALLENGES IN FORTNITE, IT WAS ABOUT TIME THAT A SKIN CAME ALONG THAT MADE YOU FEEL LESS LIKE A DANCING DAD AND MORE LIKE...WELL, A DISCO DIVA. Not only will you look really funky cutting shapes in this gold, shiny getup, but you also get a shimmering Disco Ball Back Bling thrown in for good measure. Now the dance party never has to stop!

FACT
Disco Diva first appeared on the Item Shop at the very end of 2018—what better way to dance in the new year?

"I REALLY, REALLY ENJOY THIS SKIN!"
HOLLOW, YOUTUBE

GET DOWN

FUNK OPS

INTRODUCED IN: SEASON 2
RARITY: EPIC

IF YOU LOVE TO MAKE A SCENE WHEN TEARING UP THE DANCE FLOOR, THE FUNK OPS OUTFIT WAS CREATED JUST FOR YOU. Deck yourself out with a golden, glittery shirt and boots evocative of a disco ball. The glasses and voluminous hair top it off for a look that'll stop everyone in their tracks.

SPARKLE SPECIALIST

INTRODUCED IN: SEASON 2
RARITY: EPIC

DISCO FEVER IS A SERIOUS AFFLICTION IN THE WORLD OF FORTNITE. It only takes a few minutes before you'll see someone busting out some dance moves on the battlefield. Protect yourself against all things dance-related with the very shiny Sparkle Specialist, an Outfit custom-built for boogieing. If you've ever wanted to look like a mirror ball on legs, now is your chance!

FROZEN LEGENDS
COOL NEW VERSIONS OF OLD FAVORITES

FROZEN RAVEN

INTRODUCED IN: SEASON 7
RARITY: LEGENDARY

IF YOU DIDN'T THINK RAVEN COULD GET ANY COOLER, IT LOOKS LIKE YOU WERE WRONG. The icy highlights turn it into more of a Jack Frost-ish look—perfect if you're the kind of trickster who likes to pepper the map with traps, or simply for chilling out down in the frigid bottom corner of the island.

FROZEN LOVE RANGER

INTRODUCED IN: SEASON 7
RARITY: LEGENDARY

EVERYONE'S FAVORITE LIVING STATUE IS NOW EVERYONE'S FAVORITE LIVING ICE SCULPTURE! Spread the love with this chilly Cupid costume, which even comes with an icy version of the popular Love Wings Back Bling. Love Ranger is a massively iconic Outfit, so it's nice to have an alternative if your love of the original starts to melt away.

FROZEN RED KNIGHT

INTRODUCED IN: SEASON 7
RARITY: LEGENDARY

YOU'RE NOT GOING CRAZY—FROZEN RED KNIGHT ISN'T ACTUALLY RED AT ALL. Gone is the angry black-and-red palette of the original, replaced with this slick blue-and-silver look that makes the Outfit appear more majestic than menacing. Most knight costumes were exclusive to the Battle Pass back in Season 2, so it's great to get more options. If you enjoy playing Squads as a full battalion of noble knights, this is a sure-fire way to stand out from all the other peasants.

FACT

The Frozen Legends Pack was a blink-and-you'll-miss-it bundle, available for just two weeks from late December 2018.

GARAGE BAND
FOR THOSE ABOUT TO ROCK, WE SALUTE YOU

SYNTH STAR & STAGE SLAYER

INTRODUCED IN: SEASON 5
RARITY: EPIC

BATTLE TO BE THE LAST PERSON STANDING, OR BATTLE OF THE BANDS? Why not both? The Synth Star rock-star skin focuses on retro glam, with neon colors and leather. Huge sunglasses and the fishnet glove scream 1980s rock. For Stage Slayer, it's all about attitude, with sunglasses and an outlandish top hat completing this hard-rocking style. Go all out with the Keytar or Kick Drum Back Bling and get the band back together to drop with flair.

KEYTAR

GETAWAY GANG
WHEN A DEAL IS GOING DOWN, DON'T DRESS LIKE A JOKER

SUITED UP

WILD CARD

INTRODUCED IN: SEASON 5
RARITY: LEGENDARY

AN ALREADY UNIQUE LOOK THAT CAN BE PERSONALIZED FURTHER WITH SELECTABLE STYLES. This sleek white-suited skin features decals on the mask based on the four playing card suits. Choose Clubs, Spades, Hearts, or Diamonds, then mix and match as a squad, or coordinate to flush out the opposition.

THE ACE

INTRODUCED IN: SEASON 5
RARITY: EPIC

MOST FORTNITE OUTFITS ARE UNLOCKED VIA THE BATTLE PASS OR THE ITEM SHOP, MAKING THOSE OBTAINED VIA OTHER MEANS HIGHLY DESIRABLE. This unique criminal mastermind look was only available for a limited time as part of a Starter Pack set, and these are replaced periodically to include new Outfits and cosmetics.

SWAG BAG

GINGERBREAD
SWEET COSTUMES WITH BAKED-IN HOLIDAY CHEER

GIDDY GUNNER

GINGER GUNNER

INTRODUCED IN: SEASON 2
RARITY: EPIC

IF MRS. CLAUS HAD AN EVIL ALTER EGO, IT JUST MIGHT BE GINGER GUNNER. A person-sized gingerbread woman baked to life, this hard-to-find skin is all Christmas cheer, candy, and goodwill...at least at first glance. When Ginger Gunner and her male counterpart returned in 2018, they even had brand-new "burnt" selectable styles!

FACT
As a strictly seasonal treat, Ginger Gunner appeared on the Item Shop nine times in December 2017, then just four times in December 2018. Will she be back? Log in this winter to find out!

56

COOKIE CUTTER

MERRY MARAUDER

INTRODUCED IN: SEASON 2
RARITY: EPIC

NOTHING SAYS JINGLE BELLS LIKE A SWEET DOSE OF HOLIDAY COOKIE REVENGE.
Suit up with this sugar-laced tribute to festive baked goods and let everyone on the naughty list know what happens when you forget to leave cookies out for Santa.

SUPER STRIKERS!

SOCCER STARS BRING WORLD CUP MANIA TO FORTNITE

WHEN ONE OF THE GOAL-SCORERS IN THE FINALS OF THE BIGGEST GLOBAL TOURNAMENT IN ALL SPORTS USES A FORTNITE CELEBRATION, YOU KNOW THAT THIS IS CLEARLY THE MOST POPULAR THING ON EARTH. It feels like every major soccer star is spending their downtime practicing their building, teaming up for Squads, or just practicing their Floss for the next time they hit the back of the net.

To celebrate the amazing sporting spectacle that was the 2018 World Cup, Fortnite introduced eight Goalbound Outfits, each with a different pattern and character, and all totally customizable with the colors of your favorite nation. Take them to the soccer field for a few goals!

SUPER STRIKER

INTRODUCED IN: SEASON 4
RARITY: RARE

STALWART SWEEPER

INTRODUCED IN: SEASON 4
RARITY: RARE

POISED PLAYMAKER

INTRODUCED IN: SEASON 4
RARITY: RARE

DYNAMIC DRIBBLER

INTRODUCED IN: SEASON 4
RARITY: RARE

CLINICAL CROSSER

INTRODUCED IN: SEASON 4
RARITY: RARE

AERIAL THREAT

INTRODUCED IN: SEASON 4
RARITY: RARE

WHAT'S YOUR NUMBER?
The first truly customizable skin

You can choose any number for the back of your shirt with the Goalbound set, from 01 to 99. Pick the shirt number of your favorite soccer star, or just select one at random—it's totally up to you!

FINESSE FINISHER

INTRODUCED IN:
SEASON 4
RARITY: RARE

MIDFIELD MAESTRO

INTRODUCED IN: SEASON 4
RARITY: RARE

CHOOSE YOUR FLAG!

Each Goalbound skin has its own pattern, but the color scheme can be changed by jumping into the Locker and picking from one of 32 variants—one for each of the nations that competed in the 2018 World Cup.

GREEN CLOVER
SAINT PATRICK WOULD BE PROUD

POT O' GOLD

SGT. GREEN CLOVER

INTRODUCED IN: SEASON 3
RARITY: UNCOMMON

THIS OUTFIT IS ALL ABOUT THE LUCK OF THE IRISH, BRINGING CHEERY VIBES AND GOOD FORTUNE TO ANYONE WHO DONS THIS LEPRECHAUN-LIKE SKIN. It's charming on its own, but when combined with the rest of the Green Clover set, it's an even more formidable selection. From the tiny top hat to the striped socks, this Outfit is worth tracking down.

"WHEN YOU'RE RUNNING, MONEY ACTUALLY FALLS FROM THE POT!"
ASURAHH, YOUTUBE

GRIM MEDICINE
LEECHES SOLD SEPARATELY

ARCANUM

PLAGUE

INTRODUCED IN: SEASON 6
RARITY: EPIC

WELL, THAT'S DEFINITELY A LOOK!
Based on the practical outfits of medieval plague doctors, this beaked beauty comes with all manner of curious concoctions in his apron, which might explain why his eyes are glowing like that.

SCOURGE

INTRODUCED IN: SEASON 6
RARITY: EPIC

WHILE VERY SIMILAR TO ITS MALE COUNTERPART, SCOURGE IS SOMEHOW EVEN MORE SUBTLE AND SUBDUED IN ITS DESIGN. Trading work apron and cape for trench coat and a medicine rack helps the two Outfits stand apart from each other, as does the slightly less pronounced "beak" on the mask here.

COVEN CAPE

HACIVAT
EPIC THROWS A CULTURAL CURVEBALL

HACIVAT

INTRODUCED IN: SEASON 5
RARITY: EPIC

IN PROBABLY THE MOST OBSCURE SKIN YET, HERE'S AN OUTFIT BASED ON AN ANCIENT TURKISH SHADOW-PUPPET PLAY. He's styled in traditional Turkish attire based on the models originally created for the shows. Likely added to celebrate Ramadan in Turkey and Greece, it's another great Outfit that shows off a little real-world culture.

FACT
It is believed the Karagöz and Hacivat play dates back to the 16th century. Who would have thought it would end up in Fortnite?

JUMPSHOT

INTRODUCED IN: SEASON 4
RARITY: RARE

ONE OF THE BEST CHALLENGES IN FORTNITE WAS SHOOTING HOOPS AROUND THE MAP. Did you have the nerve to shoot some while in the very middle of a match? It's just another great example of the game's originality and creativity. And what better Outfit to play ball in than Jumpshot?

TRIPLE THREAT

INTRODUCED IN: SEASON 4
RARITY: RARE

SLAM-DUNK THE OPPOSITION! The Triple Threat skin is perfect for all wannabe ballers everywhere. Wear your team's colors with pride and go dunk.

RAGNAROK

INTRODUCED IN: SEASON 5
RARITY: LEGENDARY

IF YOU SEE SOMEONE WEARING THE FEARSOME RAGNAROK OUTFIT, YOU KNOW THEY PUT THE TIME IN DURING SEASON 5. It's a scary skin, like some sort of frightening battle god, and if you manage to rack up even more XP, you can unlock the various extra style tiers for this Outfit, all the way up to this intimidating masked figure.

VALKYRIE

INTRODUCED IN: SEASON 5
RARITY: LEGENDARY

JUST AS RAGNAROK OPENED THE FIFTH SEASON WITH A BANG, VALKYRIE WAS ON HAND TO CLOSE IT WITH ONE. This is part of the growing trend for having alternatives to Battle Pass Outfits available from the Item Shop, offering players who miss out on the unlockable versions some form of consolation prize. Valkyrie is a winged warrior ready to swoop into battle and guide the fallen to the afterlife, just like her mythological Norse namesake would do.

VALKYRIE WINGS

FACT
Valkyrie was one of the last Outfits to be released in Season 5, with Ragnarok's female counterpart arriving less than a week before the start of Season 6!

CLUEFINDER

GUMSHOE

INTRODUCED IN: SEASON 4
RARITY: EPIC

IT MIGHT NOT BE THE MOST PRACTICAL COSTUME, BUT THAT DOESN'T STOP GUMSHOE FROM BEING ONE OF THE SHARPEST OUTFITS IN THE GAME. Everyone loves a good hat, and Gumshoe's pointed fedora is just about as good as it gets. Add in the pinstripe pants and the suspenders, and you have a timeless look that was fashionable back in the 1940s, and it's just as good today.

FACT
Each of these Outfits comes with its own Back Bling—go ahead and mix and match the Evidence Bag, Confidential Case, and Cluefinder options!

NOIR

INTRODUCED IN: SEASON 4
RARITY: EPIC

GRIEFERS BEWARE! Sure, the Noir skin doesn't quite give you the power to bring bad guys to justice (despite the nifty Wanted poster hanging out of the coat pocket), but you'll sure look the part. It oozes cool and harkens back to the classic age of black-and-white detective fiction, fedora and all.

MAGNIFYING AXE

SLEUTH

INTRODUCED IN: SEASON 4
RARITY: EPIC

IF NOIR IS TOO SERIOUS A LOOK FOR YOU, YOU MIGHT PREFER THIS PLAYFUL ALTERNATIVE. The brighter colors create a more casual look, and the band-aids on the face give the impression that he might not always do things by the book. But so long as you get the job done, that's all that matters, right?

DAZZLE

INTRODUCED IN: SEASON 3
RARITY: RARE

THE DAZZLE SKIN COMES WITH THE DESCRIPTION OF "THE DOMINATOR OF DUSTY DEPOT." But as we all know, that big ol' meteor had something to say about that, turning the Depot into a Divot, and the map has never been the same again, leaving poor old Dazzle here without a place to call home. Who knows... maybe she'll dominate the Divot just like her old stomping ground?

HYPERION

INTRODUCED IN: SEASON 2
RARITY: RARE

IT IS SAID, IN FORTNITE LEGEND, THAT HYPERION IS AN OUTFIT BASED ON THE GLADIATOR OF GREASY GROVE—A LEGENDARY WARRIOR. If true, then that Gladiator wore a natty headband and a cool vest. If you're the type of player who likes to look good on the battlefield, then Hyperion might be the kind of Outfit that suits you down to the ground. Very stylish, and not too outlandish.

HYPER

ICE BRINGER

THE ICE KING

INTRODUCED IN: SEASON 7
RARITY: LEGENDARY

THE FACE OF SEASON 7, WHICH IS A LITTLE STRANGE BECAUSE THIS MONARCH DOESN'T ACTUALLY HAVE A FACE! That creepy cowl shows only a pair of glowing eyes, with blue phantasmal energy leaking from them to make this Outfit even more menacing. As the top-tier reward for fully completing the Battle Pass, this imposing Outfit isn't all that common to see, which is probably just as well—it's absolutely terrifying!

THE ICE QUEEN

INTRODUCED IN: SEASON 7
RARITY: LEGENDARY

APPARENTLY, THE ICE KINGDOM IS LARGE ENOUGH TO REQUIRE TWO RULERS. The queen isn't quite as intimidating as her other half, but she still doesn't look like she'll put up with any nonsense. The spiked crown is perhaps what gives this Outfit such a commanding feel—it's just an armored winter gown without it, but those towering horns leave no doubt as to who is in charge. Enemies will be frozen with fear when you rock either of these stunning Outfits, so give them a try!

WINTER'S THORN

JAILBIRD
IT'S ONLY A CRIME IF YOU GET CAUGHT

RAPSCALLION

INTRODUCED IN: SEASON 4
RARITY: EPIC

MOST CRIMINALS ARE AT LEAST SOMEWHAT SUBTLE IN THEIR APPROACH, BUT THIS PAIR OF NE'ER-DO-WELLS WEAR THEIR STRIPES WITH PRIDE. The classic cartoon crook costume stands out in its monochrome simplicity, and there's no better way to let other players know that you're up to no good than to don a stripy top, a face mask, and a black beanie.

BURGLE BAG

SCOUNDREL

INTRODUCED IN: SEASON 4
RARITY: EPIC

THE SCOUNDREL GIVES YOUR AVATAR THAT CARTOON THIEF LOOK, PENCIL MOUSTACHE AND ALL. The set also includes the Burgle Bag and Strongbox Back Blings, the Starry Flight Glider, and the Nite Owl Harvesting Tool.

KRAMPUS
YOU DON'T WANT TO BE ON HIS NAUGHTY LIST

KRAMPUS'S LITTLE HELPER

"THIS THING IS OUT OF THIS WORLD!"
HOLLOW, YOUTUBE

INTRODUCED IN: SEASON 7
RARITY: LEGENDARY

GIVE IT UP FOR THE COOLEST VERSION OF SANTA CLAUS EVER, PUN ABSOLUTELY INTENDED.

Krampus makes jolly ol' Saint Nick look like a joke with its icy blue tongue, chains, and horns, but it's the backstory that'll make you shudder. The Outfit takes inspiration from a German folk tale based on scaring children who had been naughty rather than nice.

LAOCH
MAKE WAY FOR SOME HISTORICAL HEROES

BATTLE HOUND

INTRODUCED IN: SEASON 3
RARITY: LEGENDARY

THE STUNNING BATTLE HOUND IS ABOUT AS SCARY AS YOU CAN GET, BUT ALSO BEAUTIFUL AND HIGHLY SOUGHT AFTER. You'll see just how much you freak out your opponents when you surprise them wearing this helmet. Its piercing green eyes make a lasting impression.

BUCKLER

SILVER FANG

HIGHLAND WARRIOR

INTRODUCED IN: SEASON 3
RARITY: EPIC

IF YOU WANT THAT GLADIATOR VIBE BUT FEEL LIKE THE BATTLE HOUND'S MASK IS A STEP TOO FAR, THIS SIMPLER VERSION OF THE LOOK COULD BE THE ONE FOR YOU. The set takes its name from an old Gaelic word for "hero" or "warrior," and these Outfits certainly live up to those titles!

DARK BOMBER

INTRODUCED IN: SEASON 6
RARITY: RARE

SEASON 6 WAS ALL ABOUT CORRUPTION.
While this was most apparent from the
major changes to the map, even characters
weren't safe from the influence of the Cube.
Brite Bomber was affected the most, and
this is her corrupted alter-ego. Her eyes give
off the same ominous glow as the Cube, and
her outfit is adorned with familiar runes—if
you ever find yourself missing the mystery
of Season 6 and its six-sided secrets, this
Outfit serves as a perfect reminder.

DARK BAG

FALLING WITH STYLE

MAKE AN ENTRANCE IN THE COOLEST WAY POSSIBLE WITH THESE GLIDERS

YOUR CHOICE OF GLIDER CAN SAY A LOT ABOUT YOU AS A FORTNITE PLAYER. Are you the sort of person to swing into action on something loud and announce your presence to everyone else, or do you pick something more subtle and try to drop in unnoticed? Whatever your preferred approach, here's a selection of the best Gliders for making a stylish entrance....

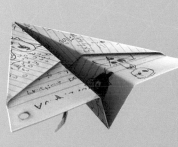

PAPER PLANE

INTRODUCED IN: SEASON 7
RARITY: RARE

Go green and fold your own Glider with this recyclable option. Don't worry—it may look flimsy, but it will hold your weight just fine.

EXTRA CHEESE

INTRODUCED IN: SEASON 7
RARITY: EPIC

A pizza box that explodes into a giant cheesy balloon to slow your descent. You might want to try using something a little less...edible.

VENUS FLYER

INTRODUCED IN: SEASON 4
RARITY: EPIC

If you want to pretend to be a bug-eating plant as you get into the fight, then look no further than this battle-hungry part of the Flytrap set.

HANG TIME

INTRODUCED IN: SEASON 4
RARITY: EPIC

Live out those hoop dreams as you dunk your way onto the battlefield and travel in some serious style. Just don't get caught double-dribbling.

HATCHLING

INTRODUCED IN: SEASON 6
RARITY: EPIC

Unlike the cute Back Bling of the same name, this creepy spider Glider is not for the fainthearted. Its animation is really quite unsettling.

THE UMBRELLA

INTRODUCED IN: SEASON 1
RARITY: COMMON

This simple Glider sends a message to other players, as you need to win a Victory Royale to earn it. Each Season offers a themed variant, too.

CRYSTAL CARRIAGE

INTRODUCED IN: SEASON 7
RARITY: RARE

Have this majestic icy unicorn guide you to the ground to add a little regal pomp to your arrival. It looks expensive, so be careful with it!

RUSTY RIDER

INTRODUCED IN: SEASON 3
RARITY: EPIC

An intimidating Glider for those who want to strike fear into their opponents' hearts as they land on a roof and start swinging their pickaxe.

DARK ENGINE

INTRODUCED IN: SEASON 6
RARITY: EPIC

All aboard! This flying ghost train was your reward if you managed to beat all the Challenges during the 2018 Fortnitemares event.

OKTOBERFEAST

INTRODUCED IN: SEASON 6
RARITY: RARE

If you often find yourself getting hungry as you glide into action, why not deck out your Glider with all kinds of delicious snacks?

ORBITAL SHUTTLE

INTRODUCED IN: SEASON 3
RARITY: EPIC

Not unlike the Deep Space Lander, but more of a classic shuttle design. One for the slightly older spacefarers out there, perhaps.

SHADOW PUPPET

INTRODUCED IN: SEASON 5
RARITY: EPIC

Do you like to put on a show? Then check out this awesome Glider, complete with an animated scene on the large sail, and its own music!

CYCLONE

INTRODUCED IN: SEASON 5
RARITY: EPIC

A sweet hi-tech hoverbike that sort of looks like somebody took a motorcycle apart and couldn't remember how to put it back together.

FLAPPY

INTRODUCED IN: SEASON 6
RARITY: RARE

The happiest Glider you will ever have the joy of seeing. The colorful Googly is a great alternative if you missed out on this PS Plus exclusive.

FIELD WRAITH

INTRODUCED IN: SEASON 6
RARITY: EPIC

This haunted scarecrow will carry you into battle and creep out opponents while looking cool, which sounds like a win/win to us.

FLYING SAUCER

INTRODUCED IN: SEASON 5
RARITY: EPIC

A saucy little number for anyone who wants a Victory Royale to go. Don't blame us if you start to feel a bit hungry after using it, though....

HOT RIDE

INTRODUCED IN: SEASON 5
RARITY: LEGENDARY

Show up to the gig in this sweet ride from the Garage Band set—one of only a handful of Legendary Gliders in the whole game!

AIRLIFT

INTRODUCED IN: SEASON 5
RARITY: EPIC

We're not sure this is proper use of emergency hardware. Still, there's no denying that this medical chopper makes for a sweet Glider!

SUGAR CRASH

INTRODUCED IN: SEASON 4
RARITY: RARE

Players with a sweet tooth will love this candy-coated Glider. It's the perfect choice for anyone who uses the Zoey Outfit regularly.

WINTER'S THORN

INTRODUCED IN: SEASON 7
RARITY: RARE

Make sure the Ice Queen rides in style with this sharp, frosty sled. Reindeer sold separately...but how does it even fly without them?

ZEPHYR

INTRODUCED IN: SEASON 2
RARITY: RARE

If you're feeling colorful, then you could do a lot worse than this crazy pattern. One for those looking to express themselves in combat.

FLAPPY FLYER

INTRODUCED IN: SEASON 6
RARITY: RARE

Sometimes, you want to be subtle in your approach. Other times, though, you just want to swing into action from beneath a giant chicken.

HALF SHELL

INTRODUCED IN: SEASON 2
RARITY: RARE

Like hiding in bushes and avoiding conflict altogether? Then this turtle shell is probably a pretty great fit for your play style.

FORERUNNER

INTRODUCED IN: SEASON 4
RARITY: RARE

It's no surprise that Vertex's Glider is just as cool as the Legendary Outfit itself. Grab this if you want to complete the Apex Protocol set!

GET DOWN

INTRODUCED IN: SEASON 2
RARITY: EPIC

Disco fever hits the Fortnite island with this nightclub-inspired banger. Combo it with a Boogie Bomb to really get the party started!

MELLO RIDER

INTRODUCED IN: SEASON 7
RARITY: UNCOMMON

Marshmello fans, rejoice! As well as a super-cool Outfit, you can show your love for the musical mastermind with this clean, cool Glider.

STARRY FLIGHT

INTRODUCED IN: SEASON 4
RARITY: RARE

Art lovers might freak out if you tell them that you sometimes use a priceless painting as a Glider. Probably best to keep that to yourself.

ROYALE DRAGON

INTRODUCED IN: SEASON 2
RARITY: LEGENDARY

A stunning Glider to celebrate Lunar New Year. It's not often in the Item Shop, but when it does appear, you'd be crazy to miss it.

BEAR FORCE ONE

INTRODUCED IN: SEASON 2
RARITY: EPIC

One of the greatest items in Fortnite, this fluffy fella even releases an "Aw" sound effect as you descend. An essential part of any collection.

TUSK

INTRODUCED IN: SEASON 7
RARITY: UNCOMMON

A prehistoric parasail made from assorted mammoth bits. Pair it with an Outfit from the Dino Guard set to drive history experts crazy.

DYNAMO & MASKED FURY

INTRODUCED IN: SEASON 5
RARITY: RARE

LOOK CLOSELY AND YOU CAN SEE THAT THE COLOR SCHEME HERE REPRESENTS THE MEXICAN FLAG, AS LUCHA LIBRE IS VERY MUCH A PART OF MEXICAN TRADITION. In this unique form of wrestling, masks are passed down through generations, and wrestlers are never seen in public without them. Of course, you can't lose your mask in Battle Royale, so just head straight into the action. Both Dynamo and Masked Fury are gorgeous, highly coveted costumes, all shiny leather, metal spikes, and tight Spandex. Real showstoppers (and starters), to say the least!

LIBRE

LYNX

INTRODUCED IN: SEASON 7
RARITY: LEGENDARY

PLAYERS HAVE COME TO EXPECT THAT THE TIER 1 BATTLE PASS OUTFIT WILL BE AN EVOLVING ONE, BUT FEW SAW SOMETHING AS COOL AS LYNX COMING. It starts out really quite innocuous, a pretty casual getup whose standout features are the cute cat ears on that reversed baseball cap.

Very quickly, though, it becomes clear that the look is going to change significantly, with its first new step ditching all bar the jacket in favor of a hi-tech bodysuit.

FACT

The real-life lynx has four different subspecies, ranging from the relatively small bobcat—common to the US—as the smallest, to the significantly bigger Eurasian lynx, Europe's third-largest predator.

By the next step, the transformation into radical techno-kitty is almost complete, but earning more XP and completing Challenges allows you to further customize the look with some vivid new color schemes.

Lynx's final form is well worth striving for, the awesome panther-like style being both cool and practical. With some progressive Outfits, you may end up using only the final forms but with Lynx, you'll want to keep using all of them!

CALAVERA

DANTE

INTRODUCED IN: SEASON 6
RARITY: EPIC

THIS REGAL COSTUME LIVES UP TO ITS EPIC STATUS EVEN BEFORE IT STARTS TO GLOW. But when it does, the skull-and-bones accents light up and you become a sharp-dressed skeleton ready to party Día de Muertos away in style. It's hard to pass up that amazing cape Back Bling, too....

ROSA

INTRODUCED IN: SEASON 6
RARITY: EPIC

CELEBRATE THE DAY OF THE DEAD ANY TIME YOU LIKE WITH THIS STRIKING COSTUME. The lacy look and elaborate face paint is cool on its own, but it also has a reactive element to it—perform well in a game and the Outfit will start to glow in the dark, its skeletal features accentuated and its neon colors popping. Perfect for anyone who isn't afraid to make their presence known!

SIX STRING STRIKER

I EON GLOW

CAN'T STOP RAVING? YOU'RE IN GOOD COMPANY HERE....

GLOW STICK

LITESHOW

INTRODUCED IN: SEASON 4
RARITY: UNCOMMON

TAKE THE SPIRIT OF THE RAVE WITH YOU WHEREVER YOU GO WITH THIS NEON-LACED COSTUME DECKED OUT WITH GLOWING RAINBOW COLORS. It's all topped off with dark sunglasses with neon-yellow Xs, letting you take to the neutral-toned vistas of Fortnite and live it up, strutting your stuff right into a Victory Royale.

NITELITE

INTRODUCED IN: SEASON 4
RARITY: UNCOMMON

ONE FOR ALL THE DANCERS OUT THERE. If you're a Fortnite raver who likes to spend as much time in the Emote wheel as you do building bases and blasting enemies, then Nitelite is probably the Outfit for you. The set also includes the Glow Rider Glider and the Glow Stick Harvesting Tool—grab the lot and you'll be able to keep the party going all night long!

RAVAGE

INTRODUCED IN: SEASON 5
RARITY: LEGENDARY

THIS FEMALE SKIN IS ONE TO SPOOK YOUR ENEMIES. The glowing eyes, the sharp talons, and tattered feathers give off a menacing vibe. The pointed beak is reflected in the Harvesting Tool, Iron Beak, and the Dark Feathers Contrail makes your journey from Battle Bus to island a flight to remember.

RAVEN

INTRODUCED IN: SEASON 3
RARITY: LEGENDARY

THUNDER CRACKS IN THE DISTANCE. CLOUDS GATHER OVERHEAD. A murder of crows squawks and takes flight. It's all very ominous. Raven is one of the most popular skins in the game. It just oozes a unique kind of dark mystery.

IRON BEAK

DUSK WINGS

DUSK

INTRODUCED IN: SEASON 6
RARITY: EPIC

SO VAMPIRES CAN APPARENTLY WALK AROUND IN BROAD DAYLIGHT NOW, ESSENTIALLY MEANING WE'RE ALL DOOMED. Celebrate the rise of our new undead overlords with this bold gothic look, just as suited to a night out at a metal gig as it is to ruling over the entire human race.

SANCTUM

INTRODUCED IN: SEASON 6
RARITY: EPIC

BECOME A CREATURE OF THE NIGHT WITH THIS NEAT VAMPIRE-STYLE COSTUME. Other players don't have to worry about getting bitten thanks to that muzzle-style mask. Watch out for players with garlic breath—the stakes are high in a Battle Royale match, after all!

NORSE

**FOR WHEN YOU WANT TO BE
MORE LOKI THAN LOW-KEY**

HUNTRESS & MAGNUS

INTRODUCED IN: SEASON 5
RARITY: EPIC/LEGENDARY

**HUNTRESS KICKSTARTED THE
SEASON 5 BATTLE PASS, WITH VIKING
WARRIOR MAGNUS HITTING THE ITEM
SHOP JUST A FEW DAYS LATER.** They
make an intimidating double act,
especially when you drop in near the
Viking village that popped up on the
map that same season, looking to
reclaim what is rightfully yours!

**ENDURING
CAPE**

TOOLS OF THE TRADE

THE BEST HARVESTING TOOLS YOU CAN COLLECT AND EQUIP IN FORTNITE

AH, THE HANDY PICKAXE—WHERE WOULD YOU BE WITHOUT IT? Whether you're using it as a last-stand weapon against another crazed player coming in for some melee fun, or applying it to chisel away and mine for some much-needed materials, your trusty Harvesting Tool is always by your side. Which is your favorite?

PARTY ANIMAL

INTRODUCED IN: SEASON 2
RARITY: EPIC

A keg of Slurp Juice on a pole, but not at all as useful for healing as that sounds. Still, when it's time to party, this pickaxe will party hard....

TRUSTY NO. 2

INTRODUCED IN: SEASON 3
RARITY: EPIC

When you tell people to "eat lead," that usually refers to bullets, right? This take on the good ol' pencil takes that saying and reinvents it.

DISCO BRAWL

INTRODUCED IN: SEASON 2
RARITY: EPIC

Make materials dance right into your pockets with this repurposed dance-floor decoration. For those who like to gather in style.

EVA

INTRODUCED IN: SEASON 3
RARITY: EPIC

The EVA—or Extra-Vehicular Axe—is a multi-articulated device that's just as adept at holding onto your materials as it is at extracting them.

THUNDER CRASH

INTRODUCED IN: SEASON 6
RARITY: EPIC

When Brite Bomber was corrupted, her axe turned to the dark side as well. But is it still a unicorn if it has three horns now?

ONSLAUGHT

INTRODUCED IN: SEASON 4
RARITY: EPIC

Unrelenting and unstoppable, this is the kind of axe you'd probably pick if you were the final boss of a dungeon in a big, bad RPG.

TOOTH PICK

INTRODUCED IN: SEASON 2
RARITY: RARE

Do you know how many sharks the maker of this axe had to catch to craft this thing? Just one—it was a really big shark!

BITEMARK

INTRODUCED IN: SEASON 3
RARITY: EPIC

You can really take a bite out of the competition with this one. The fearsome and legendary power of a T. Rex's jaws, remade just for you.

SCRAMBLER

INTRODUCED IN: SEASON 6
RARITY: UNCOMMON

An oversized kitchen tool might not be the obvious choice, but we were surprised by how well it managed to beat the competition....

SPELLSLINGER

INTRODUCED IN: SEASON 6
RARITY: RARE

Add a touch of magic to your gathering with this weird wand. It swirls with energy, but sadly isn't able to cast any useful spells on enemies.

RAINBOW SMASH

INTRODUCED IN: SEASON 3
RARITY: EPIC

People say that friendship is magic, but they won't be saying that when you start whacking them with this colorful unicorn-on-a-stick!

PLUNJA

INTRODUCED IN: SEASON 2
RARITY: RARE

Do you ever just look at two household items you've got lying around and think, *You know what? Together, they'll make a great pickaxe!*

PINK FLAMINGO

INTRODUCED IN: SEASON 1
RARITY: EPIC

Why wouldn't you want to smack things around with a pair of bright-pink tropical flamingos? Don't worry—they're not real birds!

CARROT STICK

INTRODUCED IN: SEASON 3
RARITY: RARE

A truly egg-cellent weapon, this 24-carrot tool is ideal for anyone who wants to stop other players rabbiting on about how great they are.

TAT AXE

INTRODUCED IN: SEASON 2
RARITY: RARE

Don't take it to heart, but we have an inkling that this axe might not age too well. Sure, you may want it now, but will you feel the same in 30 years?

DRAGON AXE

INTRODUCED IN: SEASON 2
RARITY: RARE

Breathe a sigh of relief if you manage to get your claws on this—you'll be on fire and you won't have to wing it to get Victory Royales anymore.

SQUID STRIKER

INTRODUCED IN: SEASON 7
RARITY: RARE

Whoever thought to use the razor-sharp beak of an alien squid as a Harvesting Tool was as smart as they were cruel. Other options are for suckers!

TENDERIZER

INTRODUCED IN: SEASON 4
RARITY: RARE

Pleased to meat you! The Tenderizer is a weapon for real butchers—definitely one for people who like to play with their food.

CHOMP JR.

INTRODUCED IN: SEASON 2
RARITY: EPIC

Rumour has it this shark was impaled on that harpoon when it was flung out of a massive tornado. We find that very easy to believe.

AC/DC

INTRODUCED IN: SEASON 2
RARITY: EPIC

Are you ready to rock the world with this shocking implement? Unleash this crackling option to electrify your opponents.

VISION

INTRODUCED IN: SEASON 7
RARITY: RARE

How do you make a spiky shovel even scarier? You stick a single working eye on it, of course! The way it blinks and looks around is super creepy....

VICTORY LAP

INTRODUCED IN: SEASON 4
RARITY: UNCOMMON

Take the wheel and use this fancy rod to get into pole position. A stick like this can really make victories fall right into your lap.

MAGNIFYING AXE

INTRODUCED IN: SEASON 4
RARITY: RARE

Hmm, what's this? Elementary, my dear player! A curious tool that looks more useful for sniffing out clues than it is for battle.

PROPELLER AXE

INTRODUCED IN: SEASON 4
RARITY: RARE

Take this axe for a spin and it should all be plain sailing for even the most inexperienced pilots. It's sure to propel you to a Victory Royale!

ICE POP

INTRODUCED IN: SEASON 7
RARITY: RARE

Frozen treats aren't usually used to smack materials out of cars and buildings, but it's oddly effective. Try to win before it melts, though.

ANARCHY AXE

INTRODUCED IN: SEASON 3
RARITY: RARE

Axes like these were originally custom-built in the markets of London, but soon, all the big corporations were copying them and they sold out.

AUTOCLEAVE

INTRODUCED IN: SEASON 4
RARITY: RARE

This pneumatic drill can penetrate the toughest materials—whether that's the Earth's crust or just someone's really thick skull.

RENEGADE ROLLER

INTRODUCED IN: SEASON 4
RARITY: EPIC

Splat your opponents and paint the town red with this practical tool. Typically used for creating rather than destroying, but you do you.

T-SQUARE

INTRODUCED IN: SEASON 7
RARITY: UNCOMMON

What's the best way to make sure something is perfectly flat? Hit it until there's nothing left! No axe says "get on my level" quite like this....

GLOBAL AXE

INTRODUCED IN: SEASON 3
RARITY: EPIC

You've got the whole world in your hands. Okay, a small, delicate world originally made for educational use, but it still breaks things just fine!

CRACKABELLA

INTRODUCED IN: SEASON 7
RARITY: EPIC

IF YOU WANT TO LOOK LIKE SOMETHING OUT OF A CHRISTMAS FAIRY TALE, CRACKABELLA IS THE OUTFIT FOR YOU.
This is one of the most detailed Epic Outfits available in the game, one with a royal grandeur that might make all but the best players take a knee in admiration. To complete the Nutcracker look, make sure you pop on the toy soldier Back Bling, Snackshot.

SNACKSHOT

CRACKSHOT

INTRODUCED IN: SEASON 2
RARITY: LEGENDARY

WHEN ASKED ABOUT HIS FAVORITE FORTNITE OUTFITS, NINJA EXPLAINED THAT HE LOVES SKINS THAT TRULY TRANSFORM YOUR CHARACTER INTO SOMETHING ELSE— THE ONES THAT DON'T JUST LOOK LIKE A CHARACTER WEARING A COSTUME. Crackshot, this bizarre wooden soldier, is a fantastic example of this, and that's why you can see Ninja playing with this skin in many of his streams. It's an amazing piece of design, and is guaranteed to freak out opponents on the battlefield.

FACT
Rumor has it that Crackshot's design is based on a nutcracker the game's art director used to see in a candy shop as a child.

BIRDSHOT

OBLIVION
EVERY GOOD HERO NEEDS AN EQUALLY BAD VILLAIN

OBLIVION

INTRODUCED IN: SEASON 4
RARITY: LEGENDARY

WITH SEASON 4 GOING HEAVY ON THE SUPERHERO IMAGERY, THIS OMINOUS SKIN FIT IN PERFECTLY. Sporting a sleek, black exterior and an orange visor, Oblivion is for those who want to look cool and who have an uncontrollable desire for world domination. That always helps. The arrival of the Outfit even coincided with rumors of a certain Season 5 rocket launch, which boosted its popularity considerably.

DESTABILIZER

FACT
Oblivion is designed to be the dark counterpart to the more heroic Criterion, whose bright colors make it clear that he's the good guy in this story....

HEIDI

INTRODUCED IN: SEASON 6
RARITY: EPIC

RELEASED AT THE END OF SEPTEMBER 2018, HEIDI CELEBRATES OKTOBERFEST IN STYLE. The costume is based on the German festival, delivering a fancy green hat, long socks, and pigtails. One of the first new skins introduced in Season 6, this comes with the Pretzel Protector Back Bling—a giant stein filled with delicious pretzels.

CLOCKWORKS

PRETZEL PROTECTOR

LUDWIG

INTRODUCED IN: SEASON 6
RARITY: EPIC

YOU'VE GOT TO LOOK YOUR VERY BEST WHEN YOU'RE GETTING GEARED UP TO GUZZLE GALLONS OF GROG. This unique spin on traditional German design comes equipped with snazzy accessories (including its very own belt-mounted tankard), but it's that perfectly styled beard that truly draws your gaze.

OMEGA
ALL GOOD THINGS MUST COME TO AN END

OMEGA

INTRODUCED IN: SEASON 4
RARITY: LEGENDARY

TOP-TIER BATTLE PASS OUTFITS WILL ALWAYS BE STATUS SYMBOLS IN FORTNITE—PROOF OF SERIOUS DEDICATION TO THE GAME THAT WILL STRIKE FEAR INTO THE HEARTS OF LESS DEVOTED PLAYERS. Few among them are quite as imposing as Omega, however, and the final evolution of its style is one of the most intimidating Outfits in the whole game.

It's the evil version of the Tier 1 skin Carbide, and even though its increasingly armored variants look very similar to Carbide's, the pitch-black coloring and neon-orange accents help to differentiate the two.

"WOW! OH MY GOD, HE LOOKS AMAZING!"
CHIP GAMES, YOUTUBE

Omega needn't stick with the orange glow, though—unlockable styles let you change the color of the suit's accents, which is obviously most effective on the final forms of the Outfit as they have more sections that light up.

The extra armor can be unlocked by leveling up in later seasons, with an extra bonus in the form of the Onslaught Harvesting Tool available to players who are able to complete at least three Challenges. The final unlock requires Season Level 80, though, so you'll have to play a fair amount if you want to look this awesome!

ONSLAUGHT

OUROBOROS
STYLE GOOD ENOUGH TO EAT (ITSELF)

LACE

INTRODUCED IN: SEASON 7
RARITY: EPIC

THIS SET IS A CURIOUS ONE, BUT BOTH OUTFITS SURE ARE STRIKING AND ORIGINAL. Ouroboros is the name often associated with imagery of a serpent eating its own tail—a picture you can see right there on Lace's top. The look itself is a hybrid of old and new, with Geisha-style face makeup (possibly based on the Chinese equivalent, the YiJi, given the rest of the set) offset by the punk-rock style. One thing is for sure: You'll certainly get noticed if you dress like this!

STITCHES

EQUILIBRIUM

PARADOX

INTRODUCED IN: SEASON 7
RARITY: EPIC

WOULD YOU BELIEVE US IF WE TOLD YOU THIS OUTFIT WAS A MODERN TAKE ON A CERTAIN KIND OF CHINESE ZOMBIE?
Well, it's true—the Jiangshi is commonly depicted wearing rich robes and with a paper talisman covering the face, so this blend of fashion and folklore is Epic's twist on that. The gown under Paradox's long jacket displays the same ornate symbol as Lace's top, again a reference to the set name but perhaps also to the circle of life itself? Either way, it's a unique and mysterious Outfit.

FACT
The timing of this collection's release and the Taoist imagery that permeates the Outfits and other cosmetics suggest that this fascinating set could have been Epic's novel way of celebrating Chinese New Year.

HAZARD AGENT

INTRODUCED IN: SEASON 4
RARITY: EPIC

AS METEORS RAINED DOWN MYSTERIOUS MATTER FROM SPACE ONTO THE FORTNITE MAP IN SEASON 4, THE HAZARD AGENT WAS SENT INTO THE FRAY TO INVESTIGATE AND ISOLATE ANY POTENTIAL BIOHAZARDS. With its unnatural green hue, this suit acts as a mirror to the darker male counterpart released as part of the set.

TOXIC TROOPER

INTRODUCED IN: SEASON 4
RARITY: EPIC

THE TOXIC TROOPER'S BLACK-AND-GREEN DESIGN IS IDEAL FOR BLENDING IN, ESPECIALLY AT NIGHT. Hide in a bush and you'd be almost completely hidden...if it weren't for the blinking beacon attached to the Outfit's chest. Hazard Agent and Toxic Trooper have their own Back Bling items—Contagion and Pathogen respectively—which follow the same color scheme.

OVERCLOCKED
WARNING: POWER OUTPUT EXCEEDS SAFE WORKING LEVELS

MAINFRAME

CIPHER

INTRODUCED IN: SEASON 3
RARITY: RARE

WHEN IT COMES TO DECODING THE HIDDEN WEAKNESSES OF YOUR ENEMIES, FEW THINGS LOOK THE PART QUITE LIKE THE CIPHER OUTFIT. This cyber-centric style mostly uses blacks and grays, with some striking red accents for extra good measure. A unique and futuristic look.

CIRCUIT BREAKER

INTRODUCED IN: SEASON 2
RARITY: RARE

THIS IS AN UNUSUAL SKIN BECAUSE IT FITS INTO MORE THAN ONE CATEGORY. Is it an android with that cool cybernetic eye? Is it a kind of cowboy with that attire? Maybe just a hacker with a weird taste in clothing? Whatever it is, Circuit Breaker is definitely cool. Complete the look with the Mainframe Glider and the Cutting Edge Harvesting Tool.

109

OVERSEER
VICTORY WAS ALWAYS PART OF THE PROPHECY

OMINOUS ORB

FATE

INTRODUCED IN: SEASON 4
RARITY: LEGENDARY

FATE IS A MUST FOR ANYONE WANTING TO BRING A BIT OF GOTHIC-FLAVORED DRAMA TO THE BATTLEGROUND. Proving popular with content creators and players alike, this is one Fate your enemies will want to avoid meeting.

OMEN

SPLIT WING

INTRODUCED IN: SEASON 4
RARITY: LEGENDARY

EVERYONE HAS A GOTHIC SUPERHERO INSIDE OF THEM, RIGHT? Omen is for those with superpowers who don't want to draw much attention: It's a sleek, understated look that you can complete with the Battle Shroud cape Back Bling. Stare deep into those glowing eyes and see if you can resist the urge to pick this Outfit up. It really gives off a futuristic, otherworldly vibe.

PARTY PARADE
THE CIRCUS HAS COME TO TOWN

BALLOON LLAMA

NITE NITE

INTRODUCED IN: SEASON 5
RARITY: EPIC

ONE OF BATTLE ROYALE'S MOST IRONICALLY NAMED SKINS—YOU MAY NEVER BE ABLE TO SLEEP AGAIN AFTER YOU WITNESS THE TRUE FACE OF EVIL. Selectable styles let you choose just how badly you want to traumatize other players, one being a dude in a ratty old clown costume, the alternative look adding a mask that stares directly into your soul.

PEEKABOO

INTRODUCED IN: SEASON 5
RARITY: EPIC

SCARED OF CLOWNS? If so, you may not be having a great time on this page, but don't worry—we're nearly done! As with the other circus-style skin, you get to pick between two versions of this Outfit (with and without the creepy mask), so you can decide just how crazy you want to look.

BUNNY BRAWLER

INTRODUCED IN: SEASON 3
RARITY: EPIC

YES, WE SAID THAT GETTING THE JUMP ON YOUR OPPONENTS IS IMPORTANT IN FORTNITE, BUT YOU MIGHT HAVE TAKEN THOSE WORDS A LITTLE TOO SERIOUSLY. Still, you'll bounce into battle with a spring in your step in this adorable getup. Military data offers no conclusive proof as to the combat effectiveness of animal-themed onesies, so get out there and do the research for yourself—you might find you're pleasantly surprised with the results.

FACT

Unlike other seasonal Outfits, Bunny Brawler has been featured on the Item Shop just as many times outside of the Easter period as it has during it.

CARROT STICK

RABBIT RAIDER

INTRODUCED IN: SEASON 3
RARITY: EPIC

RABBIT RAIDER IS A BIT OF A CLASSIC AMONG STREAMERS AND CONTENT CREATORS. On closer inspection, this option is a little scarier than he seems. That white hockey mask on his face isn't exactly the friendliest look, and you quickly realize this isn't a real rabbit at all, but instead another Fortnite warrior looking for some action on the battlefield. Combine this Outfit with emotes such as Flippin' Sexy or Star Power for maximum effect.

FACT

Both of these Outfits come with a pair of cute bunny slippers, so you're essentially getting three rabbits for the price of one. Bargain!

EGGSHELL

PIZZA PIT
CHEESY COSTUMES FOR TOPPING THE LEADERBOARDS

NIGHTSHADE

INTRODUCED IN: SEASON 6
RARITY: EPIC

THE FEMALE COUNTERPART TO THE EVER-POPULAR TOMATOHEAD OUTFIT. Nightshade's more subdued palette takes the friendly pizza parlor mascot and twists it into something much more sinister. Don't worry about the oversized mask—your head hitbox is no larger using this Outfit than any other, so enemies won't be getting easy headshots!

TOMATOHEAD

INTRODUCED IN: SEASON 3
RARITY: EPIC

PUT A SMILE ON YOUR FACE WITH THIS MOUTHWATERING OUTFIT. Tomatohead was updated in Season 5 with an alternate style that features a crown of crooked utensils and customized suit. In order to unlock its full splendor, the player had to complete three challenges.

SPECIAL DELIVERY

BLUE STRIKER

INTRODUCED IN: SEASON 4
RARITY: EPIC

ANOTHER CONSOLE EXCLUSIVE JOINS THE BATTLE, THIS TIME REPRESENTING PLAYSTATION. The Outfit itself is surprisingly understated, which only makes that strange headgear stand out even more—it almost looks like a cross between a DualShock 4 controller and a PlayStation VR headset, so it's perfect for an Outfit awarded to subscribers of Sony's PSN service.

FACT
What happened to PS Plus Pack #1, you ask? Well, the first bundle contained the Blue Team Leader Outfit, which wasn't considered part of any set, and these packs are regularly cycled out, like the Twitch ones.

BLUE SHIFT

HOLLOWHEAD

INTRODUCED IN: SEASON 6
RARITY: EPIC

HALLOWEEN IS A TIME FOR GETTING DRESSED UP IN OUTLANDISH COSTUMES, AND THEY DON'T COME MUCH WILDER THAN THIS. Stake your claim on the throne of the Pumpkin King with this grim, battle-ready costume—a ragged black combat suit topped off with a jack-o'-lantern head that spits cool blue fire. There's no room for subtlety with a look like this, although just imagine all the candy you'll get on your trick-or-treating rounds!

FACT
Hollowhead uses the same body as the Raven outfit, retooled and dyed jet black, and with the feathers restyled as autumn leaves. Bet you were too busy looking at the head to even notice!

JACK GOURDON

INTRODUCED IN: SEASON 6
RARITY: EPIC

WHILE WE'RE NOT SURE IT'S POSSIBLE TO LIKE PUMPKINS TOO MUCH, JACK HERE MAKES A PRETTY GOOD CASE FOR IT. It's one thing to stick one on your head, but quite another to don an entire pumpkin-themed suit. If you love pumpkins—like, *really* love pumpkins—then you and Mr. Gourdon should get on like a barn on fire.

PATCH PATROLLER

INTRODUCED IN: SEASON 6
RARITY: UNCOMMON

THE PERFECT WAY TO GET INTO THE HALLOWEEN SPIRIT ON A BUDGET. Eagle-eyed fans might notice that this is a pretty heavily modified version of one of the default Outfits, although there's so much going on here that it's not entirely obvious at first. If you're not fond of pumpkin heads, this scarecrow-esque bandit might be exactly what you're looking for.

RACER ROYALE
FROM POLE POSITION TO PODIUM PLACINGS

CHECKER

WHIPLASH

INTRODUCED IN: SEASON 3
RARITY: UNCOMMON

LOVE CARS? Then why not get reckless in style while dressed like an actual race-car driver? This Outfit is covered in checkered accents, which should match all of your first-place finishes. Round out your look by lapping other free-falling players with the Checker Glider.

CABBIE

INTRODUCED IN: SEASON 7
RARITY: UNCOMMON

IF YOU NEED TO GET SOMEWHERE IN A HURRY, CABBIE IS YOUR GO-TO GUY. Sporting the same checkered flag motif as his female counterpart, this is a bright and bold look that lets others know that you're ready and raring to get behind the wheel.

RANGED RECON
PRACTICAL GARB FOR GOING THE DISTANCE

SIGHT SLING

INSIGHT

INTRODUCED IN: SEASON 7
RARITY: RARE

SNIPERS TEND TO HAVE A PRETTY GOOD HANDLE ON HOW NOT TO BE SEEN. It's a pretty important skill in that line of work, yet one that Insight seems happy to ignore in the name of fashion. Still, there's no denying that turquoise camo looks cool....

SCOPE SATCHEL

LONGSHOT

INTRODUCED IN: SEASON 7
RARITY: RARE

WHILE INSIGHT TAKES LIBERTIES WITH HIS COVERT COSTUME, LONGSHOT COMES CLOSER TO GETTING CAMO RIGHT. If you enjoy picking off opponents from a distance, this sniper skin is one of the best Outfits to show others how you like to play. Fingers crossed you manage to find a Sniper Rifle!

119

FABLE

INTRODUCED IN: SEASON 6
RARITY: EPIC

WITH IT BEING PART OF THE RED RIDING SET, YOU DON'T NEED TO BE AN EXPERT ON FAIRY TALES TO KNOW WHICH FAMOUS STORY FABLE IS REFERENCING. The beauty of this Season 6 Battle Pass unlock, though, comes when it is paired with its Tier 100 bigger brother, Dire. Now you can finally see who would win in a Battle Royale match between Red Riding Hood and the Big Bad Wolf. (The smart money is on Red.)

FABLED CAPE

GUIDING GLOW

FACT

The whole of this cool fantasy set was obtained via Season 6's Battle Pass, meaning fairy tale fans who missed it may never get to Grandma's house now!

RESCUE PATROL
EVEN HEROES NEED A DAY OFF SOMETIMES...

SUN STRIDER

INTRODUCED IN: SEASON 5
RARITY: RARE

THAT VISOR MIGHT BE A LITTLE MISLEADING—IF YOU SEE SUN STRIDER RUNNING TOWARD YOU DURING BATTLE, THE LAST THING SHE IS GOING TO DO IS HELP! This off-duty lifeguard has done enough rescuing people from dangerous situations for one day, and likes to wind down by putting people *in* them instead. Hey, everyone needs to have a hobby.

RESCUE RING

SUN TAN SPECIALIST

INTRODUCED IN: SEASON 5
RARITY: EPIC

IF YOU EVER FOUND YOURSELF IN A SPOT OF TROUBLE ON THE BEACH, YOU'D WANT SOMEONE THAT LOOKS LIKE SUN TAN SPECIALIST TO COME TO YOUR RESCUE. With a long rope slung around his body, this lifeguard is ready for action, while the slap of sun cream on his nose will make sure you don't get sunburned while running around the island. The Rescue Patrol set also features the Rescue Ring and Pool Party Back Blings, the Splashdown Glider, and the Rescue Paddle Harvesting Tool.

POOL PARTY

CUDDLE TEAM LEADER

INTRODUCED IN: SEASON 2
RARITY: LEGENDARY

THERE IS JUST SOMETHING SO MAGICAL ABOUT PLAYING AS A GIANT PINK TEDDY BEAR. Everyone wants to love you, and yet you're just as dangerous as anyone else. Just who is crazy enough to step out into a Battle Royale wearing a giant pink teddy bear suit? You, that's who! And you just grabbed a Victory Royale. Who wants a hug?

FACT
The Cuddle Team Leader pairs very well with the Star Power emote for the ultimate cuteness combo. Try it and fall in love.

LOVE WINGS

LOVE RANGER

INTRODUCED IN: SEASON 2
RARITY: LEGENDARY

A BATTLE ROYALE IS ALL ABOUT DEFEATING OTHER PEOPLE. But the Love Ranger has a different motivation—he's more concerned with bringing people together. Don't be fooled by this facade, or things will go from bad to worse. After all, too much love can kill you!

TAT AXE

LUG AXE

BURNOUT

INTRODUCED IN: SEASON 3
RARITY: EPIC

THERE'S A LOT TO BE SAID FOR MAINTAINING ANONYMITY IN A BATTLE ROYALE SETTING. When foes can't see your face, you're effectively an emotionless machine racing toward them. Sure, that fancy racing helmet won't actually protect you from damage, but that's not what it's there for this time....

CYCLONE

REDLINE

INTRODUCED IN: SEASON 5
RARITY: EPIC

REDLINE STRIKES US AS SOMETHING OF A RISK-TAKER. For one thing, she's ditched the padded leather riding jacket in order to show off her sweet sleeve tattoos. She's certainly not road-ready in that getup, but then she doesn't really need to be. If you're all about taking huge risks while looking as cool as possible, Redline encapsulates that attitude well.

FACT
This set is an anomaly in that the Item Shop Outfit actually came out before the Battle Pass one—it usually tends to happen the other way around.

DOWNSHIFT

SHARP STYLE
CASUAL, COOL, AND CONTEMPORARY

RHINESTONE RIDER

FORTUNE

INTRODUCED IN: SEASON 5
RARITY: RARE

FORTUNE RADIATES A SENSE OF ATTITUDE AND SWAGGER. While it might not be as visually loud as the male counterpart, Fortune's subtle use of gold dog tags and aviator sunglasses demonstrates that it's possible to have a practical Outfit that doesn't compromise on style.

MONIKER

INTRODUCED IN: SEASON 5
RARITY: RARE

IF YOU SAW SOMEONE DRESSED LIKE MONIKER IN REAL LIFE, YOU MIGHT THINK THEY LOOKED PRETTY COOL. Fortnite's designers clearly had the same thought, as this is part of the Sharp Style set. Combine these skins with the Studded Axe and Rhinestone Rider for maximum sharpness.

SHOGUN
FIGHT WITH HONOR, WIN WITH SKILL

BLADED WINGS

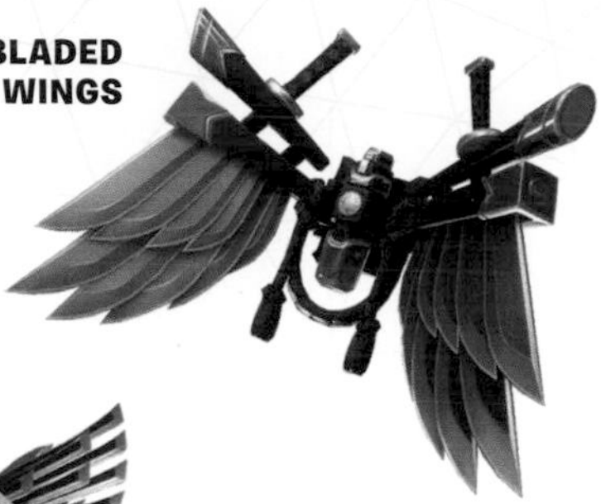

KABUTO

SHOGUN

INTRODUCED IN: SEASON 6
RARITY: LEGENDARY

EMBRACE YOUR INNER SAMURAI WITH THIS ELABORATE AND EVOCATIVE OUTFIT. The ornate demon-faced helmet is the most striking part of the ensemble, although the gold-rimmed armor pads and engraved panels make it a spectacle whichever part should catch your eye first. The other pieces of the set reinforce the intimidatingly cool ancient Japanese style.

SKULL TROOPER

INTRODUCED IN: SEASON 1
RARITY: EPIC

A TRUE FORTNITE CLASSIC, SKULL TROOPER HAS BEEN A MAINSTAY FOR BIG STREAMERS AND CONTENT CREATORS SINCE IT MADE ITS DEBUT DURING THE FIRST FEW WEEKS OF THE BATTLE ROYALE MODE GOING LIVE. Its slightly ridiculous but seriously awesome design showed players that Fortnite wasn't going to be a completely serious action game—it was going to have a lively personality, too.

FACT
The bone-chilling Skull Trooper completely disappeared from the Item Store between Seasons 1 and 6, adding to its rarity value.

GHOST PORTAL

SKULL RANGER

INTRODUCED IN: SEASON 6
RARITY: RARE

WHEN SKULL TROOPER FINALLY RETURNED TO THE ITEM SHOP, HE BROUGHT A FRIEND. Skull Ranger is the iconic Outfit's female counterpart, yet it's only a Rare rather than an Epic so it's a little cheaper to add to your collection. Both now come with selectable styles, letting you either rock the classic look or light things up with a UV version.

SKY STALKER
SURVIVING ON A WING AND A PRAYER

SKY STALKER

INTRODUCED IN: SEASON 4
RARITY: LEGENDARY

CHANNEL YOUR INNER CLASSIC FIGHTER PILOT WITH THIS THROWBACK OUTFIT.
Its understated coat with muted colors, coupled with the striking green gas mask, is evocative of the kind worn around World War II. The Sky Stalker set also includes the Legendary Back Bling Last Gasp, which is a pair of oxygen tanks. The entire look works best when coupled with the Propeller Axe, which, strangely enough, isn't part of the set.

FACT
Promotional materials for the Sky Stalker skin featured a character hanging off the Battle Bus with one arm and holding a Propeller Axe in the other.

SOLID STEEL
YOU CAN'T KILL THE METAL...THE METAL WILL LIVE ON

SOLID STRIDER

CHROMIUM

INTRODUCED IN: SEASON 4
RARITY: RARE

IF WE'RE GIVEN THE CHANCE TO PLAY AS SOME KIND OF FUTURISTIC HUMANOID WAR MACHINE, YOU'D BETTER BELIEVE WE'RE GOING TO TAKE IT! Chromium would be a pretty tame Outfit if it weren't for the fact that she's got metal skin and glowing eyes, but that just makes the plain clothes feel that much more striking.

DIECAST

INTRODUCED IN: SEASON 4
RARITY: RARE

IF YOU IGNORE THE MASSIVE CHROME MAN AND LOOK AT THE CLOTHES HE'S WEARING, YOU MIGHT NOTICE THAT THEY ARE ALMOST EXACTLY THE SAME AS THE SCOUT'S. Outside of the beret and a different color choice, they are near identical—was he dropped into a vat of liquid metal on his way to the hat store?

DARK MATTER

DARK VOYAGER

INTRODUCED IN: SEASON 3
RARITY: LEGENDARY

THIS DARK ASTRONAUT COSTUME WAS ONE OF THE HIGHLIGHT OUTFITS IN SEASON 3'S BATTLE PASS, AND IT ISN'T DIFFICULT TO SEE WHY. It's almost completely black, but the neon stripes on the torso and back are so bright that they might just be visible from outer space. Although this Outfit doesn't come bundled with any Back Bling, it pairs perfectly with the Dark Matter backpack.

FACT

The Space Explorers set is one of Fortnite's largest, made up of a whopping 15 items across four different cosmetic categories!

**DEEP SPACE
LANDER**

DARK VANGUARD

INTRODUCED IN: SEASON 3
RARITY: LEGENDARY

ANOTHER GREAT EXAMPLE OF AN OUTFIT DESIGNED TO PREVENT PLAYERS FROM MISSING OUT TOO MUCH ON BATTLE PASS CONTENT. If you made it to Tier 70 and unlocked the alternate Dark Voyager, you wouldn't really need this extremely similar skin—it's more designed to help less active players live out their spacefaring fantasies.

FISH TANK

LEVIATHAN

INTRODUCED IN: SEASON 3
RARITY: LEGENDARY

WHEN IT COMES TO UNIQUE LOOKS IN FORTNITE, FEW OUTFITS SCREAM "LOOK AT ME!" MORE THAN THIS GUY. From the boots to the neck, it looks like any other spacesuit. But then you look above the collar...and see a bowl with an angry-looking fish inside. It's certainly one of the more unusual Outfits in the game.

MISSION SPECIALIST

INTRODUCED IN: SEASON 3
RARITY: EPIC

IT'S GROUND CONTROL TO MAJOR YOU WITH THIS INTERGALACTIC OUTFIT, GLEANED FROM THE FIRST TIER OF THE SEASON 3 BATTLE PASS. Suit up to head out onto the battlefield with this eye-catching Outfit. Take an even bigger leap for mankind by combining this with the EVA Harvesting Tool.

MOONWALKER

INTRODUCED IN: SEASON 3
RARITY: EPIC

THE MOONWALKER OUTFIT IS AN EYE-CATCHING SPACESUIT THAT HAS QUITE LITERALLY BEEN DESIGNED TO WALK ON THE MOON. Its design and style—from the copper-colored visor to the padded panels on the side of the body—gives the whole Moonwalker suit a proper retro feel.

ORBITAL SHUTTLE

BACKING IT UP

THERE ARE SO MANY THINGS YOU CAN COLLECT AND CUSTOMIZE IN FORTNITE. The range runs from full Outfits to tree-hacking axes, but few of these items are appreciated as much as the humble Back Bling. This being a third-person shooter, you are staring at the back of your avatar throughout every match, so why not invest in placing something awesome there to look at? Here's a rundown of some of the best options....

ENDURING CAPE

INTRODUCED IN: SEASON 5
RARITY: LEGENDARY

The Norse set brings Viking terror and Berserker rage to Fortnite, including the thick fur of the Enduring Cape. A must-have piece of gear.

OFFWORLD RIG

INTRODUCED IN: SEASON 4
RARITY: LEGENDARY

This strange cloak/backpack combo was awarded to those who managed to complete all of the Blockbuster Challenges in Season 4's Battle Pass.

CUDDLE BOW

INTRODUCED IN: SEASON 2
RARITY: LEGENDARY

Once you've bought the adorable Cuddle Team Leader Outfit, you'll have access to the giant Cuddle Bow to help wrap up any costume.

TRASH LID

INTRODUCED IN: SEASON 7
RARITY: EPIC

A makeshift shield, stolen from a trash can. If you can't find your flow and are playing like garbage, you might as well look like it, too!

DESTABILIZER

INTRODUCED IN: SEASON 4
RARITY: LEGENDARY

Forming part of the impressive Oblivion set, the Destabilizer is actually a tweaked variant of the Stabilizer Back Bling.

REMUS

INTRODUCED IN: SEASON 7
RARITY: EPIC

Call us crazy, but maybe carrying around a live wolf on your back isn't the smartest thing you can do. Just putting that out there....

RED SHIELD

INTRODUCED IN: SEASON 2
RARITY: LEGENDARY

No medieval-themed items in Fortnite look as swish as the Red Knight's crimson-colored Red Shield, replete with an intimidating crest.

ROYALE FLAGS

INTRODUCED IN: SEASON 2
RARITY: LEGENDARY

Released just three days before the end of Season 2, the impressive Royale Flags are part of the three-piece Wukong set.

SCALY

INTRODUCED IN: SEASON 3
RARITY: LEGENDARY

The Scaly Back Bling makes you look like a dinosaur. Surely you don't need a reason to use it beyond that? Of course you don't.

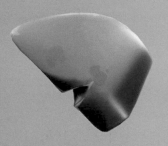

SHARK FIN

INTRODUCED IN: SEASON 5
RARITY: LEGENDARY

Want to show other players how tough you are? Flag yourself as an apex predator by wearing this shark fin on your back.

SIX STRING

INTRODUCED IN: SEASON 3
RARITY: LEGENDARY

The hard-rocking Six String brings some angular and neon-pink style to your spine. Strap it on and get ready to turn the action up to 11!

BONESY

INTRODUCED IN: SEASON 6
RARITY: EPIC

Fortnite's very first Pet and a certified Good Boy. Like all Pets, Bonesy reacts to how you play, so make sure you don't let him down!

STABILIZER

INTRODUCED IN: SEASON 4
RARITY: LEGENDARY

The red-and-blue Stabilizer—unlocked with the Criterion Outfit—offers a colorful alternative to the darker Destabilizer Back Bling.

SNOWBRAND

INTRODUCED IN: SEASON 7
RARITY: EPIC

Only a fool rushes into a fight without a weapon. But it takes an even greater fool to rely on a weapon that doesn't work, like this decorative blade.

BLACK SHIELD

INTRODUCED IN: SEASON 2
RARITY: LEGENDARY

The Black Shield Back Bling is part of the Fort Knights set, and was available as part of the Battle Pass along with its owner, the Black Knight.

ASTRO

INTRODUCED IN: SEASON 3
RARITY: EPIC

This retro Back Bling could only be achieved by reaching Tier 47 of Season 3's Battle Pass, along with a bunch of other space-themed goodies.

BACK PLATE

INTRODUCED IN: SEASON 5
RARITY: EPIC

Become the snazziest target on the battlefield with this set of '80s weights that will make you a smash hit. They're not too heavy, are they?

BALLISTIC

INTRODUCED IN: SEASON 5
RARITY: EPIC

This little item has a cool, biker-style look to it with its leather texture and ultra-dark aesthetic. The golden bullets are a neat touch.

LAST GASP

INTRODUCED IN: SEASON 4
RARITY: LEGENDARY

Season 4 brought plenty of themes to Fortnite, including the retro military looks of Last Gasp. It's part of the two-item Sky Stalker set.

IRON CAGE

INTRODUCED IN: SEASON 3
RARITY: LEGENDARY

Quite large, but goth chic is a fair trade for being a slightly more visible target. You never know when you might need a cage full of feathers....

HAMIREZ

INTRODUCED IN: SEASON 7
RARITY: EPIC

Show your fluffy hamster friend a bit of the outdoor world by strapping her to your back. Just try not to get her shot, okay?

CRESTED CAPE

INTRODUCED IN: SEASON 3
RARITY: LEGENDARY

A super-exclusive item. You can only acquire Crested Cape once you've bought the Battle Hound Outfit—a rare visitor to the Item Shop.

DARK MATTER

INTRODUCED IN: SEASON 3
RARITY: LEGENDARY

The Dark Matter Back Bling is part of the Space Explorers set, which includes the sci-fi Dark Void spinal accessory. Mix and match your tech!

LOVE WINGS

INTRODUCED IN: SEASON 2
RARITY: LEGENDARY

Introduced at the end of the game's second season, the Love Wings Back Bling features a pair of large stone wings. No, you can't fly.

BOOMBOX

INTRODUCED IN: SEASON 5
RARITY: EPIC

Mullet Marauder is one of the loudest skins in Fortnite. Make it even louder with the Boombox—guaranteed to make you stand out.

RAPTOR SATCHEL

INTRODUCED IN: SEASON 2
RARITY: LEGENDARY

With its shovel, water canister, and line pull, the Raptor Satchel has a proper Air Force feel about it. Its coloring is also awesome.

CAMO

INTRODUCED IN: SEASON 6
RARITY: EPIC

Okay, trying to get a chameleon to lend you its color-changing properties was a smart idea. Too bad it didn't work out, though.

MERTANK

INTRODUCED IN: SEASON 4
RARITY: LEGENDARY

There's something fishy about this Back Bling. So fishy, its battered scuba-kit look has been paired with the cute-yet-scary Moisty Merman Outfit.

HATCHLING

INTRODUCED IN: SEASON 3
RARITY: LEGENDARY

Unleash your inner dinosaur in Fortnite with the prehistoric style of the Hatchling, part of the colorful Dino Guard set. Don't forget to feed it!

SHACKLED STONE

INTRODUCED IN: SEASON 7
RARITY: LEGENDARY

Remember that mysterious cube that roamed the map? Now you can keep a piece of that memory with you always. Just be careful with it....

AEROBIC ASSASSIN

INTRODUCED IN: SEASON 5
RARITY: EPIC

BURN CALORIES AND TAKE DOWN ENEMIES AS AN AEROBIC ASSASSIN, INSPIRED BY THE ADVENTURE IN FASHION THAT WAS THE 1980s. This retro throwback look features bold colors and lightning-bolt designs that would look perfect in any gym. The legwarmers, sweatbands, and oversized sunglasses complement the look and evoke a vibe from the old days. Everything on this skin yells "larger than life"— especially that hair!

AXERCISE

MULLET MARAUDER

INTRODUCED IN: SEASON 5
RARITY: EPIC

LOOKING LIKE HE JUST STEPPED OUT OF A TIME MACHINE, THE MULLET MARAUDER IS A TRIP BACK TO THE DECADE OF PASTEL HUES, SHOULDER PADS, AND HUGE HAIR. It's the latter that gives the skin its name—it's business in the front, party in the back—but let's not ignore the tracksuit, based on fashions that were popular everywhere during the 80s. Back then, it was cool to carry around giant stereos blasting music, which explains the Boombox Back Bling. Perhaps this guy is heading to the gym and needs a little musical motivation....

BOOMBOX

FACT
Most boomboxes played audio cassettes, which were cheap and easy to copy, but lacked in playback quality next to vinyl.

WINDBREAKER

145

BLASTING CAP

FIREWORKS TEAM LEADER

INTRODUCED IN: SEASON 4
RARITY: EPIC

SOMETIMES WHEN YOU CELEBRATE, YOU JUST HAVE TO GO ALL-OUT. For times like these, you need an Outfit such as the Fireworks Team Leader—the all-American mascot of blowing things up in the name of independence. If you thought that Cuddle Team Leader couldn't get any more garish, you thought wrong. This multi-colored spectacle will stick out from a mile away on the battlefield, so only those brave or skilled enough to deal with that kind of attention should consider dressing up like this.

STAR-SPANGLED RANGER

INTRODUCED IN: SEASON 4
RARITY: UNCOMMON

WORRIED THAT FULL FLAG-PRINT CLOTHES MIGHT BE SEEN AS OVERKILL? Never fear—this red, white, and blue outfit lets you fly your colors with a touch of class. Its clean design makes it fine to bust out on any occasion. Like the set's male equivalent, this is a cool and understated option, especially when compared to that bright-blue beast across the page!

STAR-SPANGLED TROOPER

INTRODUCED IN: SEASON 4
RARITY: UNCOMMON

CELEBRATE YOUR INDEPENDENCE WITH THIS STRIKING LOOK. Want to stand out while still remaining relatively low-key? Slink around the battlefield in this slick getup. This patriotic ensemble is one-fourth of the Stars and Stripes set, which includes the fireworks-themed Back Bling and two female Outfits. If you can't be the adorable Fireworks Team Leader, then at least try to spice things up with this affordable and attractive alternative.

MIDNIGHT OPS

INTRODUCED IN: SEASON 3
RARITY: RARE

DON'T LET THE NAME FOOL YOU—THIS GUY IS JUST AS EFFECTIVE DURING THE DAY AS HE IS IN THE MIDDLE OF THE NIGHT. This set's black-and-red motif makes for a strong and striking look. These two even have their own pickaxe, the cool-looking Spectre.

SHADOW OPS

INTRODUCED IN: SEASON 2
RARITY: EPIC

PRACTICAL FOR ANY SITUATION WHERE YOU NEED TO SNEAK INTO AN ENEMY BASE UNDETECTED. Catching your enemies by surprise and eliminating them efficiently makes you feel like a highly trained secret agent, which is exactly what this slick Outfit is designed to represent.

SPECTRE

STORM FUSION
ALWAYS TAKE THE WEATHER WITH YOU

DEVASTATOR

INTRODUCED IN: SEASON 2
RARITY: UNCOMMON

PLAIN DOESN'T NEED TO BE BORING. The Devastator skin doesn't have any flashy gadgets or a fancy mask, but it does have angled decals and patchy camo patterns which evoke future fighting. For some reason, it also has two belts, just in case your trousers are weighed down from all those Boogie Bombs. Smart!

PULSE AXE

DOMINATOR

INTRODUCED IN: SEASON 2
RARITY: UNCOMMON

THE FEMALE VERSION OF THE DEVASTATOR OUTFIT. The lower body is where the two are a little different, with Dominator's asymmetrical armor plating making this a surprisingly intricate design for an Uncommon Outfit.

RENEGADE RAIDER

INTRODUCED IN: SEASON 1
RARITY: RARE

BACK IN FORTNITE'S SEASON 1, THERE WAS ONE SUIT EVERYONE WANTED TO ADD TO THEIR LOCKER—RENEGADE RAIDER. With its WWI-style flight cap and goggles, rust-colored tank top, and football-esque face paint, the Outfit takes some inspiration from classic comic-book character designs. It's also yet to return to rotation since Season 1!

RUST LORD

RUST BUCKET

INTRODUCED IN: SEASON 3
RARITY: EPIC

LIVING OFF WASTELAND SCRAPS DOESN'T SOUND LIKE OUR IDEA OF A GOOD TIME, BUT THIS GUY SEEMS TO MAKE IT WORK. That spiked helmet should make others think twice about looting on your turf, and the general look is that of someone you probably don't want to mess with. Observant fans might notice that he has the Unreal logo emblazoned on his jacket.

HAY MAN

FIELD WRAITH

INTRODUCED IN: SEASON 6
RARITY: EPIC

THERE'S SOMETHING PRETTY UNNERVING ABOUT SCARECROWS, AND IT DOESN'T HELP WHEN THEY'RE RUNNING AROUND WIELDING AUTOMATIC WEAPONS. Creep out your rivals with this peculiar patchwork person, brought to life by some kind of dark magic, or maybe just by the sheer boredom of standing still in a field all day and all night.

HAY NEST

STRAW OPS

INTRODUCED IN: SEASON 6
RARITY: EPIC

JUST BECAUSE YOU'RE DESIGNED TO SCARE BIRDS DOESN'T MEAN YOU HAVE TO LOOK RATTY. Straw Ops rocks a pretty cool dress, although you'll be too busy looking at those eerie glowing eyes and her sewn-up mouth to really notice. It's a less scruffy look than that of the male version, and the sunflowers are a good way to take a bit of the edge off.

BRITE BOMBER

INTRODUCED IN: SEASON 2
RARITY: RARE

WITH LOTS OF COLOR AND SOME AMAZING UNICORN ART, THIS IS ONE FOR WHEN YOU WANT TO MAKE AN IMPRESSION. The unicorn theme runs through the Sunshine & Rainbows set, which includes the Brite Bag Back Bling, Rainbow Smash axe, and Rainbow Rider Glider. The Pool Party Back Bling—an inflatable unicorn—also works well with the other items in this set.

RAINBOW SMASH

BRITE GUNNER

INTRODUCED IN: SEASON 3
RARITY: EPIC

DID YOU GROW UP WEARING T-SHIRTS WITH CARTOON CHARACTERS ACROSS THEM? Do you, like us, continue to do so long into adulthood? If so, the Brite Gunner skin will likely resonate with your inner child. As the name suggests, it's not exactly a subdued look, rather one for when you want to explode onto the scene in all your glory.

BRITE BAG

FACT
Why does Brite Gunner cost more than Brite Bomber? Well, it comes bundled with the Brite Bag Back Bling—the perfect thing to cap off either skin!

SUPPORT SQUADRON
THE SKILLS TO PAY THE MEDICAL BILLS

FIELD SURGEON

INTRODUCED IN: SEASON 5
RARITY: EPIC

MAN DOWN! "MEDIC!" WILL BE THE CALL YOU WAIT TO HEAR. When your squad starts asking for bandages and med-kits, why not turn up and commit to the role of support? A futuristic style is the base for this classic red-and-white look, and there's no mistaking your intent to save lives.

TRIAGE TROOPER

INTRODUCED IN: SEASON 5
RARITY: EPIC

EVERY GOOD TEAM NEEDS A SUPPORT PLAYER BACKING IT UP. Don this classy costume and that unsung hero could be you, ready to sit back and dish out heals. In this role, you'll want to fight from range as much as possible—opposing players might look to pick off a healer first and hope the rest of the team crumbles.

AIRLIFT

SUSHI
REVENGE IS A DISH BEST SERVED RAW

CHEF'S CHOICE

SUSHI MASTER

INTRODUCED IN: SEASON 5
RARITY: RARE

SUSHI CHEFS ARE KNOWN FOR THEIR PRECISION AND RESPECT FOR TIME-HONORED CUSTOMS. Inspired by Japanese culture, the Sushi Master's blue combined with white is bold and bright, while featuring bamboo accessories and rope work around the limbs.

MAKI MASTER

INTRODUCED IN: SEASON 6
RARITY: RARE

PREPARING SUSHI REQUIRES A GREAT DEAL OF SKILL AND PRECISION. As it happens, those two qualities just happen to be very useful in a Battle Royale setting as well, making these two chef Outfits great ways to tell other players that you're all about finesse...or that you just really like raw fish.

GOODIE BAG

ZOEY

INTRODUCED IN: SEASON 4
RARITY: EPIC

CANDY LOVERS REJOICE—YOUR PERFECT OUTFIT IS HERE. Zoey is a bright and playful look for anyone who wants to wear their love of all things sweet on their sleeves... literally, in this case. The hot-pink top is covered in gumdrops, peppermints, chocolates, and all kinds of other treats, and there's plenty more where those came from in the Goodie Bag Back Bling.

LOLLIPOPPER

TECH OPS
WE'RE PRETTY SURE THAT'S CHEATING....

TECH OPS

INTRODUCED IN: SEASON 7
RARITY: RARE

RARE OUTFITS JUST SEEM TO KEEP GETTING MORE AND MORE ELABORATE. This recent addition to the club is a unique and striking figure, admittedly fairly typical from the neck down but that swanky hi-tech headgear is what really makes the skin look awesome. Those four green lenses are advanced optics of some kind—they won't actually help in battle, but they sure do look good.

COAXIAL COPTER

157

TWIN TURNTABLES
SUPERSTAR DJS, HERE WE GO!

GLOW SHOW

DJ BOP & DJ YONDER

INTRODUCED IN: SEASON 6
RARITY: LEGENDARY/EPIC

THE MIGHTY DJ YONDER WAS THE HEADLINER FOR THE SEASON 6 BATTLE PASS. If you missed out but still want to run around dressed as animal DJ, never fear—DJ Bop steps away from the turntables to visit the Item Shop from time to time, so be sure to keep an eye out for her!

EQUALIZER

158

HAVOC

INTRODUCED IN: SEASON 3
RARITY: LEGENDARY

WHILE IT MAY LOOK MORE SUITED TO GUERRILLA WARFARE THAN AN IMPROMPTU DABBING SESSION, HAVOC IS A MUST-HAVE OUTFIT FOR ANYONE WHO TAKES THEIR FIGHTS SERIOUSLY. The balaclava and urban camo make it pretty clear that you're not messing around, and that's sometimes the exact message you want to send to opponents.

BACKUP PLAN

SUB COMMANDER

INTRODUCED IN: SEASON 3
RARITY: EPIC

WHEN YOU'VE BEEN COOPED UP IN AN UNDERWATER TIN CAN FOR WEEKS, IT'S ONLY NATURAL THAT YOU'D WANT TO BLOW OFF SOME STEAM. And where better to do that than on an island with dozens of other folks running around, ripe for eliminating? This is a pretty low-key look for an Epic skin, but that works in its favor pretty well.

INSTIGATOR

GALE FORCE

INTRODUCED IN: SEASON 4
RARITY: LEGENDARY

THERE WERE PLENTY OF HEROES ON CALL DURING SEASON 4, BUT THIS UNIQUE OUTFIT WAS AMONG THE HARDEST TO GET. It's a classic comic-book style, all plated armor and coordinated colors to make it look like you're ready to soar into battle. And you had better be—people will expect good things from anyone rocking a look like this!

FACT
The only harder hero to unlock in Season 4's Battle Pass was Omega— the final unlock of the whole thing!

VANISHING POINT
FOR MAKING YOUR ENEMIES DISAPPEAR

OVERTAKER

INTRODUCED IN: SEASON 5
RARITY: EPIC

WITH THAT KATANA STRAPPED TO HIS BACK, MAYBE UNDERTAKER WOULD HAVE BEEN A MORE SUITABLE NAME FOR THIS MASKED MENACE. It's a bold and mysterious look, one ready to get the job done without revealing a thing about the person behind the visor. That's probably for the best, really...

IGNITION

WHITEOUT

INTRODUCED IN: SEASON 5
RARITY: EPIC

IS THIS SKIN SUPPOSED TO REPRESENT GOING OUT FOR A RIDE ON A MOTORBIKE OR SKIING THROUGH THE ALPS? Likely it's the former, but either way this clean Outfit is sleek and stylish, with slightly more padding and less contrasting detail than the male equivalent.

VENTURE
GOLDEN-AGE HEROES ARRIVE TO SAVE THE DAY AGAIN

VENTURA

INTRODUCED IN: SEASON 4
RARITY: EPIC

THIS PAIR OF RETRO-STYLE SUPERHEROES COULD HAVE FALLEN RIGHT OFF THE PAGES OF ANY NUMBER OF VINTAGE COMIC BOOKS. The metallic bodysuit and prominent *V* emblem leave folks in no doubt as to who they've been rescued by, and you even get a cool cape— what kind of superhero would you be without one? If you fight for justice, the Venture set will be the best sidekick you could hope for.

VENTURA CAPE

VENTURION

INTRODUCED IN: SEASON 4
RARITY: EPIC

SOMETIMES, ONLY A SUPERHERO CAN SAVE THE WORLD. With the Venturion skin, you can be decked out in silver-and-gold spandex to stand alongside so many superstars of illustrated panel and cinema screen. Being a superhero means keeping your identity secret, which this Outfit's mask enables via goggles and breathing apparatus. Sharklike fins decorate the top, showing that you're built for speed, while the sleek gauntlet and shoulder unit add powerful flair.

TRIUMPH

SIX STRING

POWER CHORD

INTRODUCED IN: SEASON 3
RARITY: LEGENDARY

AN AWESOME OUTFIT FOR THOSE TIMES WHEN YOU NEED TO BRING A BIT OF PUNK-ROCK ATTITUDE TO A BATTLE ROYALE. If you're the type of player who likes to drop onto the Fortnite map with a lot of noise, aggression, and power, and then cause as much carnage as possible when you're down there, Power Chord may well be the skin of choice for you.

FACT
Power Chord pairs well with the Garage Band Outfits—get your supergroup together and go rock the island!

PUNCTURE PACK

MAYHEM

INTRODUCED IN: SEASON 6
RARITY: RARE

IF YOU WANT PEOPLE TO LEAVE YOU ALONE, DRESSING UP LIKE A CRAZY SCAVENGER IS A PRETTY GOOD WAY TO GO ABOUT IT. Between the spiked pauldrons and gloves, the tattered hood, and that not-strictly-necessary breathing apparatus, it's a pretty intimidating Outfit, and one likely to make foes think twice about tussling with you. That sounds like a win to us....

JUNKJET

RUCKUS

INTRODUCED IN: SEASON 6
RARITY: RARE

JUST WHEN YOU THOUGHT THIS SET COULDN'T GET ANY MORE OVER-THE-TOP, THE APPROPRIATELY NAMED RUCKUS EXPLODES INTO THE PICTURE. While Mayhem looks like she might still be finding her feet as a scavenger, this guy has been in pure bandit mode for some time. The full-face gas mask with tufts of clown-like blue hair is a horrifying combo, and we don't even want to know what's in those canisters on his chest. If you want to go full-bore raging maniac, there's no better Outfit in the game in which to do it.

FACT
Since their release, Mayhem and Ruckus have only appeared on the Item Shop a handful of times, making them highly desirable.

**COVERED
CRUSADER**

CALAMITY

INTRODUCED IN: SEASON 6
RARITY: LEGENDARY

WHETHER YOU'RE LOOKING TO ROUND UP CATTLE OR HOLD UP BANKS, THIS INCREASINGLY AWESOME COWGIRL OUTFIT IS SURE TO MOSEY ON INTO YOUR FAVORITES. Like many progressive skins, it starts out quite basic, although the ten-gallon hat and spurred boots give a fair idea of what is to come.

Calamity slowly evolves from ranch hand to hardened outlaw as you level up and complete Challenges, eventually ending up in a fetching spiked duster with a glowing trim. Being able to dial it back to something more subtle is a welcome option—it's tricky to keep a low profile when you're glowing!

Couple this look with the other Outfit in the Western Wilds set, Deadfire, and you'll be a pair of rootin'-tootin' gunslingers ready to put the "wild" into Wild West.

DEADFIRE

INTRODUCED IN: SEASON 6
RARITY: LEGENDARY

REACTIVE OUTFITS HAVE BEEN HOT FOR A WHILE NOW, AND THIS GUY WAS THE GUNSLINGER WHO KICKED OFF THE TREND.
Deadfire starts each match as a typical cowboy-style skin, but the Outfit evolves as the action goes on. As you damage and outlive other players, he gradually transforms into this undead sheriff and even bursts into weird spiritual flames if you perform well enough—the Dark Shard axe blazes up along with you, too! It's part of the Western Wilds set along with Calamity, if you want to get a posse together.

DARK SHARD

SHACKLED STONE

172

INTRODUCED IN: SEASON 4
RARITY: EPIC

WHEN YOU ROCK UP TO THE ISLAND DRESSED LIKE AN ACE FIGHTER PILOT, PEOPLE ARE GOING TO TAKE YOU SERIOUSLY. It's a strong look, and one that suggests you have plenty of combat experience—whether that's actually the case or not is irrelevant! This Starter Pack exclusive has since been cycled out in favor of newer Outfits, but if you missed it, you might want to look to the Sky Stalker or Aviation Age sets to get your pilot fix.

FACT
The Bogey Bag Back Bling may look like a parachute, but sadly, you can't use it to sail down onto the map....

**BOGEY
BAG**

KEEPING IT COOL

SURRENDER TO THE SNOW WITH SWEET STYLE STRAIGHT FROM THE SLOPES

IT CAN GET CHILLY OUT THERE ON THE BATTLEFIELD! Suit up and rep your favorite country with this selection of sweet winter-sports-centric skins in the form of the male-oriented

Alpine Ace set and the female Mogul Master selection. Whether you want to fly your flag or just head out to procure that Victory Royale in style, there's a version for you.

ALPINE ACE (CAN)   **ALPINE ACE (CHN)**   **ALPINE ACE (FRA)**   **ALPINE ACE (GBR)**

ALPINE ACE

THE SET OF ARCTIC ACE SKINS COME IN EIGHT DIFFERENT FLAVORS, INCLUDING A GENERIC "BASE" COLORING. Seven territories are represented with unique costumes—Canada, China, France, Great Britain, Germany, South Korea, and the USA—and all varieties feel equally suited to action on the slopes or anywhere else. Even if you're not into winter sports at all, these Outfits offer plenty of ways to ensure that your opponents are well aware of where you're from, so they can curse your birthplace when you scoot on by with a win. Plus, you get to wear cool goggles. Who doesn't love a fresh pair of goggles?

ALPINE ACCESSORIES (CAN)

ALPINE ACCESSORIES (CHN)

ALPINE ACCESSORIES (FRA)

ALPINE ACCESSORIES (GBR)

ALPINE ACCESSORIES (GER)

ALPINE ACCESSORIES (KOR)

ALPINE ACCESSORIES (USA)

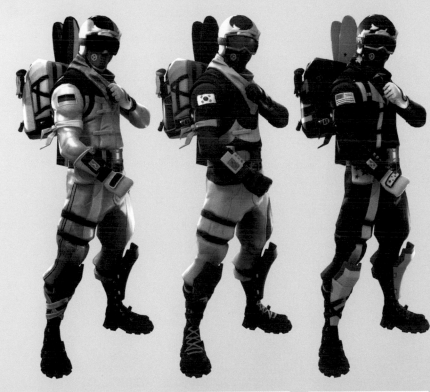

ALPINE ACE (GER)   **ALPINE ACE (KOR)**   **ALPINE ACE (USA)**

MOGUL MASTER

THE MOGUL MASTER SKINS OFFER A LITTLE SOMETHING FOR THE LADIES, AND THEY'RE A LOT MORE FORM-FITTING AND AERODYNAMIC THAN THE THICKER, BULKIER ALPINE ACE COUNTERPARTS. Like the male Alpine Ace costumes, there's a dedicated skin for seven different regions, as well as a base option for anyone who just loves winter sports. There's no mistaking which country you're repping, with the entirety of the costume featuring the nation's flag emblazoned on the front. Just be careful out there—that fetching helmet isn't going to be stopping bullets any time soon!

MOGUL MASTER (CAN) **MOGUL MASTER (CHN)** **MOGUL MASTER (FRA)** **MOGUL MASTER (GBR)**

ALPINE ACCESSORIES

DON'T GET CAUGHT WITHOUT THESE AWESOME ADD-ONS.
The Alpine Ace and Mogul Master sets aren't the only snow-themed things available for decking out your character. Check out the Alpine Accessories Back Bling selection as well, including special themed backpacks that match every single Outfit available. They round out the ensemble with a cool pair of skis, just in case you want to make like you have some downhill R&R planned for when you've wrapped up the Victory Royale.

MOGUL SKI BAG (CAN)

MOGUL SKI BAG (CHN)

MOGUL SKI BAG (FRA)

MOGUL SKI BAG (GBR)

MOGUL SKI BAG (GER)

MOGUL SKI BAG (KOR)

MOGUL SKI BAG (USA)

MOGUL MASTER (GER)   **MOGUL MASTER (KOR)**   **MOGUL MASTER (USA)**

WINTER WONDERLAND
AN ICY OPTION TO FREEZE OTHERS IN THEIR TRACKS

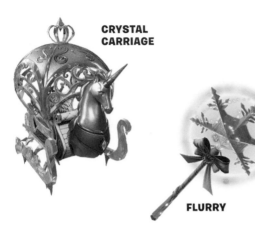

CRYSTAL CARRIAGE

FLURRY

GLIMMER

INTRODUCED IN: SEASON 7
RARITY: LEGENDARY

IF YOU WANT A LITTLE WINTER MAGIC BUT THE ICE KING AND ICE QUEEN OUTFITS ARE TOO SEVERE FOR YOUR TASTES, THIS FABULOUS ALTERNATIVE MIGHT JUST GIVE YOU CHILLS.
It's another fantastic Legendary Outfit to add to your collection, with a cool cloak Back Bling and majestic Glider to complete the costume and freeze your foes in fear. Looking this regal, you'll be hoping that any enemies that see you will take a knee and swear fealty to you rather than opening fire...but that probably won't happen.

WUKONG
DON'T MONKEY AROUND WITH INFERIOR OUTFITS

WUKONG

INTRODUCED IN: SEASON 2
RARITY: LEGENDARY

ONE OF THE ALL-TIME GREATEST SKINS IN FORTNITE HISTORY, WUKONG IS INSPIRED BY CHINESE MYTHOLOGY. It effectively lets you play as an ancient monkey god. It's a supremely ornate design and, at the time it was introduced, was an indication of the level of care and attention Epic was going to give to these special Legendary skins. This is the only Outfit in the eponymous Wukong set, but when you pick it up, you also get the Royale Flags Back Bling and Jingu Bang harvesting tool. The very definition of Legendary!

JINGU
BANG

FACT
The name Wukong comes from Sun Wukong, the name of an actual Chinese deity. Great attention to detail there!

ZENITH
PERFECTLY PRIMED FOR PEAK PERFORMANCE

ZENITH

INTRODUCED IN: SEASON 7
RARITY: LEGENDARY

SEASON 7 WAS THE START OF A GENEROUS NEW TREND IN FORTNITE, WITH THE FIRST TIER OF THE BATTLE PASS AWARDING TWO PROGRESSIVE OUTFITS RATHER THAN JUST ONE. Like the Lynx Outfit that unlocked alongside it, Zenith undergoes a transformation into something more animalistic as you earn experience and complete Challenges, with fuzzy claws growing over his gloves and the snow hood becoming a colorful mane of sorts—

ALTITUDE

one variant even gets tiger-like stripes on the suit. As with most similar skins, colors unlock separately to styles and can be mixed and matched at will, which can lead to some pretty crazy combinations once you manage to unlock the lot.

If you're planning on dropping in at Polar Peak or are just worried it might be a little cold on the island, consider this warming winter wonder as one of your go-to Outfits.

FAQs

EVERYTHING YOU NEED TO KNOW ABOUT OUTFITS AND OTHER CUSTOMIZATION ITEMS IN FORTNITE

HOW DO I GET MORE BATTLE ROYALE OUTFITS?

There are several ways to add more Outfits to your collection. Some can simply be bought with V-Bucks from the Item Shop, which cycles its content daily, while others need to be unlocked via the Battle Pass, where completing challenges and rising though the tiers each season will net you tons of cool cosmetic items. A few items can only be obtained via special promotions, so be sure to keep an eye out, both in and around the game!

WILL THE SKIN I WANT EVER BE BACK IN THE ITEM STORE?

Never say never! Some skins are extremely rare to find in the store, though, so you'll need to check in daily if you don't want to miss a particular Outfit that you've had your eye on for a while. However, skins that are tied to previous Battle

Pass rewards are unlikely to ever grace the store—they're badges of honor for those who managed to get them, so be sure to unlock those as you go or you might miss your chance forever!

HOW CAN I GET MORE V-BUCKS?

Fortnite's in-game currency, V-Bucks, can be obtained in several ways. Battle Pass owners can earn rewards by completing challenges, while the cooperative Save the World component of the game also offers V-Bucks as rewards. Finally, you can buy additional V-Bucks with real money, but never trust any external sites that offer to sell you V-Bucks or claim they can give them to you for free.

CAN I MIX AND MATCH DIFFERENT OUTFIT PARTS?

Yes and no. The clothes themselves are entire fixed outfits that can't be altered, but you're free to use any Back Bling items you've unlocked with any skin. Get creative and see what kinds of weird and wonderful mash-ups you can create to really express yourself—some of the combinations can be really out there, so go nuts!

CAN I GO BACK TO USING THE DEFAULT SKIN?

Sure, if you like! Some people like to do this to lull opponents into a false sense of security and make them think they're up against a beginner rather than someone with experience, while others just really like the starting Outfits. Either way, you still can't choose which of the eight default characters you'll get, but you can switch to the starting costume any time, just as you would any of the other skins.

DO CERTAIN OUTFITS INDICATE A LEVEL OF PLAYER SKILL?

Not necessarily. Outfits unlocked from the top tier of a Battle Pass (such as Ragnarok) certainly suggest a degree of experience and commitment, as unlocking them can take a lot of time and effort, so those are the main ones to watch out for if you're concerned that an opponent might be too tough to take on. The same is true for Outfits that were only available in earlier seasons—they're not a direct indication of player skill, but they at least show that the wearer has been playing the game for a long time, so it's likely that they know their way around the island.

SHOULD I BE CHANGING SKINS REGULARLY?

It's entirely up to you. The only Outfits that actually benefit from being used for long

periods of time are ones like Drift and Omega that evolve as you earn experience while using them. With the rest, you can change things up as often as you like to suit your mood. Stick to a personal favorite or change things up every game—it's your call!

DO THE VARIOUS GLIDERS HANDLE DIFFERENTLY?

No—just like Outfits, these items are purely cosmetic and none give any particular gameplay advantages over any others. A simple umbrella will prove just as effective as a hi-tech flying machine, so just equip whichever you like the best and soar through the sky in style.

WHAT'S THE POINT OF THE SPRAYS?

They're just for fun! Some can be used as a way of communicating simple messages (like slapping a "GG" down after a particularly epic 1v1), while others, such as the door, bush, tunnel, and window, might be able to fool less savvy opponents. There are also options for expressing yourself in other ways—as with everything, just go ahead and use the ones you like the most!

WHAT'S THE RAREST OUTFIT IN THE GAME?

There are two contenders for this title. First is the Renegade Raider, a skin that was only available way back in Season 1 and that reportedly only a few hundred people managed to unlock and buy back then, making it a real status symbol among Fortnite veterans. The other option would be the Royale Bomber, a skin that was originally only available in certain Europe-exclusive PS4 hardware bundles, making it particularly unusual to see out in the wild.

PASSING IT ON

What's the most efficient way to unlock Outfits?

While you can buy many of Fortnite's Outfits and other cosmetic items individually, the Battle Pass offers a cost-effective way to fill up your Locker without emptying your wallet of V-Bucks. You'll need to put in a good amount of play to make your way up through the Tiers and unlock all the goodies, so hop on the bus and get started!

THE CHECKLIST

WITH NEW OUTFITS BEING ADDED TO FORTNITE ALL THE TIME, IT CAN BE TRICKY TO KEEP TRACK OF ALL YOUR OPTIONS. You might have a favorite skin that you never take off, or you might just forget that you unlocked something really cool a few seasons back and never got around to breaking it in. Here's your chance to take stock of what you have—as well as what you're hoping to add to your collection soon—with a handy checklist of every skin covered in these pages, as well as where to turn to learn more about any of the featured Outfits. Grab a pen and start checking them off!

ABSOLUTE ZERO PAGE: 17	**ABSTRAKT** PAGE: 10	**AERIAL THREAT** PAGE: 60	**AEROBIC ASSASSIN** PAGE: 144	**A.I.M.** PAGE: 11
AIRHEART PAGE: 18	**ALPINE ACE** PAGE: 174	**ALPINE ACE (CAN)** PAGE: 174	**ALPINE ACE (CHN)** PAGE: 174	**ALPINE ACE (FRA)** PAGE: 174

ALPINE ACE (GBR) PAGE: 174

ALPINE ACE (GER) PAGE: 175

ALPINE ACE (KOR) PAGE: 175

ALPINE ACE (USA) PAGE: 175

ARACHNE PAGE: 14

ARCHETYPE PAGE: 16

ARCTIC ASSASSIN PAGE: 17

BACKBONE PAGE: 20

BATTLEHAWK PAGE: 8

BATTLE HOUND PAGE: 76

BEEF BOSS PAGE: 40

BLACK KNIGHT PAGE: 46

BLUE SQUIRE PAGE: 46

BLUE STRIKER PAGE: 115

BRITE BOMBER PAGE: 152

BRITE GUNNER PAGE: 153

BUNNY BRAWLER PAGE: 112

BURNOUT PAGE: 126

CABBIE PAGE: 118

CALAMITY PAGE: 170

CARBIDE PAGE: 24

CHOMP SR. PAGE: 26

CHOPPER PAGE: 20

CHROMIUM PAGE: 133

CIPHER PAGE: 109

CIRCUIT BREAKER PAGE: 109

CLINICAL CROSSER PAGE: 60

CLOUDBREAKER PAGE: 18

CRACKABELLA PAGE: 100

CRACKSHOT PAGE: 101

CRITERION PAGE: 28

CUDDLE TEAM LEADER PAGE: 124

DANTE PAGE: 88

DARK BOMBER PAGE: 77

DARK VANGUARD PAGE: 135

DARK VOYAGER PAGE: 134

DAZZLE PAGE: 70

DEADFIRE PAGE: 172

DEVASTATOR PAGE: 149

DIECAST PAGE: 133

DISCO DIVA PAGE: 48	**DJ BOP** PAGE: 158	**DJ YONDER** PAGE: 158	**DOMINATOR** PAGE: 149	**DOUBLE HELIX** PAGE: 37
DREAMFLOWER PAGE: 43	**DRIFT** PAGE: 38	**DUSK** PAGE: 91	**DYNAMIC DRIBBLER** PAGE: 59	**DYNAMO** PAGE: 84
ELITE AGENT PAGE: 21	**EON** PAGE: 42	**FABLE** PAGE: 120	**FAR OUT MAN** PAGE: 43	**FATE** PAGE: 110
FIELD SURGEON PAGE: 154	**FINESSE FINISHER** PAGE: 61	**FIREWORKS TEAM LEADER** PAGE: 146	**FLAPJACKIE** PAGE: 12	**FLYTRAP** PAGE: 44
FORTUNE PAGE: 128	**FROZEN LOVE RANGER** PAGE: 50	**FROZEN RAVEN** PAGE: 50	**FROZEN RED KNIGHT** PAGE: 51	**FUNK OPS** PAGE: 49
GINGER GUNNER PAGE: 56	**GLIMMER** PAGE: 178	**GRILL SERGEANT** PAGE: 41	**GROWLER** PAGE: 12	**GUMSHOE** PAGE: 68
HACIVAT PAGE: 64	**HAVOC** PAGE: 160	**HAY MAN** PAGE: 151	**HAZARD AGENT** PAGE: 108	**HEIDI** PAGE: 103
HIGHLAND WARRIOR PAGE: 76	**HIME** PAGE: 22	**HOLLOWHEAD** PAGE: 116	**HUNTRESS** PAGE: 92	**HYPERION** PAGE: 71

INSIGHT
PAGE: 119

JACK GOURDON
PAGE: 117

JUMPSHOT
PAGE: 65

KRAMPUS
PAGE: 75

LACE
PAGE: 106

LEVIATHAN
PAGE: 136

LITESHOW
PAGE: 89

LONGSHOT
PAGE: 119

LOVE RANGER
PAGE: 125

LUDWIG
PAGE: 103

LYNX
PAGE: 86

MAGNUS
PAGE: 92

MAKI MASTER
PAGE: 155

MASKED FURY
PAGE: 84

MAVEN
PAGE: 23

MAVERICK
PAGE: 27

MAXIMILIAN
PAGE: 19

MAYHEM
PAGE: 168

MERRY MARAUDER
PAGE: 57

MIDFIELD MAESTRO
PAGE: 61

MIDNIGHT OPS
PAGE: 148

MISSION SPECIALIST
PAGE: 137

MOGUL MASTER
PAGE: 176

MOGUL MASTER (CAN)
PAGE: 176

MOGUL MASTER (CHN)
PAGE: 176

MOGUL MASTER (FRA)
PAGE: 176

MOGUL MASTER (GBR)
PAGE: 176

MOGUL MASTER (GER)
PAGE: 177

MOGUL MASTER (KOR)
PAGE: 177

MOGUL MASTER (USA)
PAGE: 177

MONIKER
PAGE: 128

MOONWALKER
PAGE: 137

MULLET MARAUDER
PAGE: 145

MUSHA
PAGE: 22

NIGHTSHADE
PAGE: 114

NITE NITE
PAGE: 111

NITELITE
PAGE: 89

NOIR
PAGE: 69

OBLIVION
PAGE: 102

OMEGA
PAGE: 104

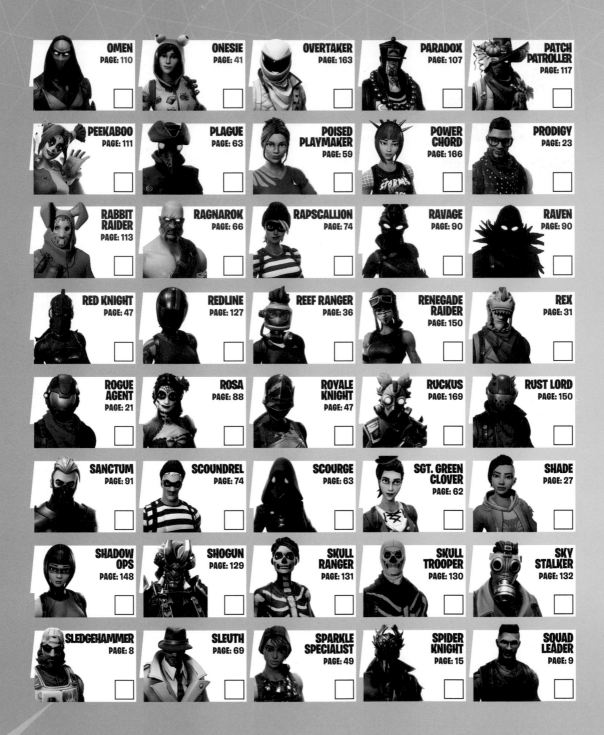

OMEN PAGE: 110	**ONESIE** PAGE: 41	**OVERTAKER** PAGE: 163	**PARADOX** PAGE: 107	**PATCH PATROLLER** PAGE: 117
PEEKABOO PAGE: 111	**PLAGUE** PAGE: 63	**POISED PLAYMAKER** PAGE: 59	**POWER CHORD** PAGE: 166	**PRODIGY** PAGE: 23
RABBIT RAIDER PAGE: 113	**RAGNAROK** PAGE: 66	**RAPSCALLION** PAGE: 74	**RAVAGE** PAGE: 90	**RAVEN** PAGE: 90
RED KNIGHT PAGE: 47	**REDLINE** PAGE: 127	**REEF RANGER** PAGE: 36	**RENEGADE RAIDER** PAGE: 150	**REX** PAGE: 31
ROGUE AGENT PAGE: 21	**ROSA** PAGE: 88	**ROYALE KNIGHT** PAGE: 47	**RUCKUS** PAGE: 169	**RUST LORD** PAGE: 150
SANCTUM PAGE: 91	**SCOUNDREL** PAGE: 74	**SCOURGE** PAGE: 63	**SGT. GREEN CLOVER** PAGE: 62	**SHADE** PAGE: 27
SHADOW OPS PAGE: 148	**SHOGUN** PAGE: 129	**SKULL RANGER** PAGE: 131	**SKULL TROOPER** PAGE: 130	**SKY STALKER** PAGE: 132
SLEDGEHAMMER PAGE: 8	**SLEUTH** PAGE: 69	**SPARKLE SPECIALIST** PAGE: 49	**SPIDER KNIGHT** PAGE: 15	**SQUAD LEADER** PAGE: 9

STAGE SLAYER PAGE: 53	STALWART SWEEPER PAGE: 59	STAR-SPANGLED RANGER PAGE: 147	STAR-SPANGLED TROOPER PAGE: 147	STRAW OPS PAGE: 151
SUB COMMANDER PAGE: 161	SUN STRIDER PAGE: 122	SUN TAN SPECIALIST PAGE: 123	SUPER STRIKER PAGE: 58	SUSHI MASTER PAGE: 155
SYNTH STAR PAGE: 53	TECH OPS PAGE: 157	TEKNIQUE PAGE: 10	THE ACE PAGE: 54	THE ICE KING PAGE: 72
THE ICE QUEEN PAGE: 73	TOMATOHEAD PAGE: 114	TOXIC TROOPER PAGE: 108	TRAILBLAZER PAGE: 9	TRIAGE TROOPER PAGE: 154
TRICERA OPS PAGE: 31	TRIPLE THREAT PAGE: 65	VALKYRIE PAGE: 67	VALOR PAGE: 162	
VENTURA PAGE: 164	VENTURION PAGE: 165	VERTEX PAGE: 13	WHIPLASH PAGE: 118	
WHITEOUT PAGE: 163	WILD CARD PAGE: 54	WINGMAN PAGE: 173	WINGTIP PAGE: 19	
WRECK RAIDER PAGE: 36	WUKONG PAGE: 179	ZENITH PAGE: 180	ZOEY PAGE: 156	

First published in the UK in 2019 by WILDFIRE
an imprint of HEADLINE PUBLISHING GROUP

Cataloguing in Publication Data is available from the British Library

Hardback 978 14722 6529 6

Design by Future plc.

Edited by Luke Albigés.

All images © Epic Games, Inc.

Printed and bound in Italy by L.E.G.O. S.p.A.

HEADLINE PUBLISHING GROUP

An Hachette UK Company
Carmelite House
50 Victoria Embankment
London, EC4 0DZ
www.headline.co.uk www.hachette.co.uk

Little, Brown and Company
Hachette Book Group
1290 Avenue of the Americas, New York, NY 10104
Visit us at hbgusa.com/fortnite

www.epicgames.com

First Edition: July 2019
First U.S. Edition: July 2019
Little, Brown and Company is a division of Hachette Book Group, Inc.
The Little, Brown name and logo are trademarks of Hachette Book Group, Inc.

ISBNs: 978-0-316-53045-3 (paper over board)
978-0-316-53044-6 (ebook), 978-0-316-42476-9 (ebook),
978-0-316-42475-2 (ebook)

U.S. edition printed in Canada

All images © Epic Games, Inc.

FRI

UK Hardback: 10 9 8 7 6 5 4 3 2 1

U.S. Paper Over Board: 10 9 8 7 6 5 4 3 2 1